Safe in Socks
My Memoir

By

Teresa Fidelis Lancaster

DEDICATION

IN LOVING MEMORY OF

My cherished mom who taught me to conquer anything
this world throws at me with grace, and always to hold my
head high, and how to bake.

My beloved dad who encouraged me to achieve my goal of
becoming an attorney to follow in his footsteps.

My dear friend Linda Trescott Watts who always had
a kind word to say about everyone and who selflessly
walked into hell to stand by my side through the horrors
at Keough.

****

To my husband Randy, my daughters: Lisa, Christy,
Annette, my brother Mark, my sister Pat, my dear friend
Jean, and all the courageous survivors of childhood
sexual abuse.

TABLE OF CONTENTS

PROLOGUE

"THE TIMES, THEY ARE A-CHANGIN'"
BY: ANNETTE WINTER SUDBROOK

As Bob Dylan's 1964 song title says: '*The Times, They Are A-Changin*', in 1968, times were indeed changing. Across the ocean, young men maneuvered the brutal, unknown jungles of Vietnam, looking death or worse in the eye. In Baltimore, hundreds of young women confronted a very different kind of battle. My mother was one of those women. Her world then was forever and dramatically changed and today, in 2021, she continues to exist as a force of change for seeking justice. In the late 60's and 70's, there were countless movements professing peace and love. Adolescents openly rejected the controlling hands of authority, with good reason.

In this climate, people explored new ways to view love, family, government, and religion. Doctrines were questioned, concepts explored, and convictions were challenged. There was a revolution, a reform of ideas, addressing human freedoms such as civil rights and equality for women. Consequently, there were transgressions. A deep and dark world of corruption, crime, and sinful abuse of power, grew. Where there is light and love, darkness and hate lurks contrasting in the shadows. In the pages of this book, you will read abhorrent abominations. In the world, a new generation of people was experiencing horrors barely imaginable.

My mother was among a group of deeply religious teens meant to be sheltered from this unpredictable and changing world. From 1968 until 1972, she attended an all-girls Catholic high school in Baltimore, Archbishop Keough. Her name is Teresa Fidelis Harris Gagne Lancaster. You might be thinking that she was safe from the chaos and sins of the changing world at Keough in the pious hands of devoted nuns and priests. Her parents thought she was. However, the experiences she endured were amongst the most heinous imaginable. Somehow, she did survive. It was not the indiscretions and sins of a world outside the religious sanctuary that she needed to suffer and overcome; it was the horrors that took place inside a supposed haven meant to protect girls from a society that was out of control.

This book is her story, the story of a young girl brought up in the strict Catholic religion, a girl who loved her faith and strived to be pious – only to have her beliefs destroyed by a monster. A girl who ended up being in the center of one of the most horrific sexual abuse rings run by a predator priest. *Safe in Socks* explores the connections between the unsolved murder of Sister Catherine Cesnik (who taught at Keough and tried to help the girls being abused there) and Father Maskell. My mom reveals her profound, darkest, and most horrifying moments of fear, pain, crime, and corruption that she experienced at the hands of a Catholic priest, enabled by his church. She also shares her moments of fortitude, inspiration and perseverance. *Safe in Socks* unfolds the events that took her from an innocent child to a victim, survivor, mother, attorney, and advocate.

CHAPTER 1

LOSING MY RELIGION

That's me in the corner

That's me in the spot-light

Losing my religion

…

Oh no I've said too much

I haven't said enough -REM

"Blessed are the pure in heart, for they shall see God."

On the very first day I was inside Father Maskell's office at Archbishop Keough High School, he sat me on his lap and systematically removed my clothes like he was unwrapping a gift. That moment is etched in my mind forever. It seemed to happen really fast but at the same time freakishly slow. His voice sounded far off and echoey as he maneuvered his immense hands to unbutton my blouse. While undressing me, he said, "Oh, there have been some very bad girls here at Keough who have said awful things about me. You would never do that, would you, Terry?" I was frozen with fear. Then, before I knew it, my blouse dropped onto the floor. I always wore an undershirt because I never liked uncomfortable bras. As Maskell slipped my undershirt up over my head he laughed. He said he bet I thought my breasts were too small. He caressed them and told me they were quite average and well-formed. My gray wool uniform skirt was next to go. I watched it drop to the floor like an old blanket. My underpants followed and landed next to his office chair. I stared at my socks, my blue knee-highs. He let me keep them on. I was so very grateful he left them on. Everything else was gone.

Feeling his monstrous hands all over my naked body put me in a different place. I could hear my heartbeat, but I seemed to be elsewhere watching Maskell caress my breasts. He said, "I'm touching you in a godly manner. Do you let your boyfriend do this?"

Suddenly, there was a knock at his office door. All I could think of was that I was naked. Maskell pushed me to the floor like a discarded rag doll as he got up to open the door. He was fully clothed in his black pants and shirt with his white Roman collar. I ran to hide, cowering on the floor in a corner out of sight. I was ashamed. I thought my heart would burst out of my chest. I could hear muffled talking at the door. God, was he going to let someone in to see this crazed girl naked in his office? Who was at the door? What would they think? What would they say?

The talking stopped. Maskell locked his door without letting in whoever was there. He saw me huddled in that corner, trying to cover myself with my hands. He laughed raucously and said, "What are you doing there? You thought I was going to let them in to see you, didn't you?" He yanked me up roughly by one arm and threw me in his chair. He ordered me to "Spread 'em!" I was no longer present in my body. The rest of that day is a blur. I don't remember jack shit.

I can't recall getting dressed. I guess he could have dressed me. Suddenly, I was sitting in the passenger seat of Maskell's car. He said he was taking me home. He walked with me up to my front door and rang the doorbell. My father opened the door and the two of them started talking. I was able to slip past my dad and run upstairs to my room.

Once in my room, I started to shake all over. What the hell had just happened? At that moment my reality shifted. I was in my safe house now but I felt ashamed, dirty, like a trapped animal. I felt confused, sad, betrayed, shocked. I felt lost.

So how did I end up in Father Maskell's office that first time, a crisp autumn morning in 1970? It started the night before.

I'd gotten home from school and was in my room listening to the Moody Blues on my small stereo. My mom yelled up the stairs and asked me to come downstairs to the kitchen. My mom was usually busy with one of my three older brothers, or talking to my dad about whatever adults talk about, or washing dishes or whatever else moms do. Entering the kitchen, I could see my mom sitting at the table. My purse was open, its contents on the table.... a brand-new hypodermic needle, a small pipe, rolling papers, and a joint.

Oh shit, I thought. I had gotten that needle from a friend of mine who's older sister was dating a medical student. She managed to get it from his medical bag for me to give a friend of mine who had hepatitis from shooting up heroin with an old dirty needle. That was definitely not my thing. I was into Boone's Farm Strawberry Wine and weed. Jesus, why did I leave that needle in my purse???

My mom looked like she'd been crying, and my dad was white as a ghost. My mom wanted answers but she couldn't even ask me questions. I had never seen her like that. I never wanted to hurt her. She was the kindest person in the whole world and I hurt her. She said her doctor would do a blood test on me and she would know everything I was doing. My dad started interrogating me like the lawyer he was. Where did I get the drugs, was it at school, who gave them to me? I felt like this most uncomfortable sad-ass drama would go on for the rest of my life. I was told I was grounded except for school and church and that I wouldn't be going to church or anyplace else with my so-called friends. I could only go out with my parents.

I'd never been in trouble before. I was a good, Catholic girl. In fact, I was pretty damn good at everything I did. I always got straight A's at my elementary school, St. William of York, and was on the girls' basketball team there. I had been a Girl Scout and made it to the Cadette level. Grades were never a problem. I was getting straight A's and was on the honor roll at what I thought was the most prestigious high school in Maryland, maybe even in the country - Keough! I engaged in multiple extra-curricular activities. I collected dolls from around the world and raised tropical fish. I took a photography class at Keough, and developed my own pictures in a darkroom I put together in my basement. I spent most of my summers at Hunting Hill's Swim Club with neighborhood friends. I was on the swim team there, one of the few who mastered the butterfly stroke. I was smart, athletic, kept my room clean, and went to Mass every Sunday.

My parents usually left me alone. Our conversations were never heated. They were proud of their baby, their only girl. I'd become so accustomed to the respected role I had in my family – I had no idea how to deal with hysterical parents.

The next morning Dad drove me to school, without our usual conversation......me talking about what college I wanted to go to and Dad insisting that I master typing and shorthand so I could be a well-paid legal secretary. Things had changed for me in many ways as I started my Junior year at Keough. My dad believed it was best for me to switch from the college prep program I had enrolled in when I started at Keough, to its comprehensive business program. He reasoned if I mastered typing, shorthand and organizational capabilities, I could easily find a job in a professional office as a legal secretary or even as a paralegal. Dad also thought, as many did back then, that I would need a husband who would take care of me and, if I worked in a reputable office, I could meet a respectable man to marry.

I agreed to pursue the business program even though I had high grades in the academic curriculum and most of my friends were college bound. I soon found home economics and the other business classes boring and unchallenging. I had a lot of free time that I used to spend studying and I guess that is why I had started to hang out with a new crowd, people who partied. Now, I found myself lumped in with "wild deviants" in the eyes of my parents.

The drive to school this particular morning was horrible. Last night's confrontation had taken a toll on my dad. He lost all his color and was visibly shaken. I never saw him so vulnerable, and it made me very, very sad. The mood was tense and heavy, not the usual relaxed banter. When I got into school, I spied my best friend Linda. I ran to her and burst into tears. I told her about the night before, how my mom went through my purse and how horrible it was. I asked her, "What can I do? My life is over. What can I do?"

Suddenly, I remembered the tour my mom and I went on before I got accepted at Keough. The tour guide said there was an on-call priest, a counselor with an office at Keough. I said, "Linda, the priest, the priest! He is supposed to help girls with problems, with whatever they need here at Keough." I told Linda that my dad would believe a priest... that I could ask the priest to call my dad and tell him that I'm not a lost cause. He could smooth this mess out. Let's go ask the priest for help. Even though it was time for our first class, Linda stood by me. Hand in hand we walked down the long hallway that led to the chaplain's office. I didn't even know his name. I read it on the door: Father A. Joseph Maskell. Great, his name is Joseph, just like my dad's. I had found a way out, I thought…

Maskell did some taking that day. He took away my future, my perception of the world, my identity, my sense of self, my innocence. I shifted. I fell off a cliff and tumbled for years. After the abuse was over, I tried to find myself again. That day marked the beginning of a new reality. Feelings of safety and security were forever altered. I was changed forever. But as time went on, I found that whatever changed in me made me stronger, made me never give up. And that change was a good thing. I was going to survive.

CHAPTER 2

LITTLE FLOWER

What's in a Name?

I grew up in a traditional Catholic home with three older brothers. All of us were named after saints, persons whom the Catholic Church recognizes as having exceptional holiness and closeness to God. Catholics pray to saints to intercede with God on their behalf and to help them with special needs. I was taught that non-Catholics who didn't carry the name of a saint were to be pitied.

My oldest brother was named after Saint Joseph, the husband of the Blessed Virgin Mary. He knew that Mary was pregnant with someone else's child before he married her. According to scripture, an angel appeared to Saint Joseph in a dream and told him to take Mary as his wife and that the baby she carried was from the Holy Spirit. Faithfully, Saint Joseph did as he was told and became the legal father of Jesus. It is an honor to carry his name. The Feast Day of Saint Joseph is celebrated on March 19.

My second brother was named after Saint Blase, a physician. It is noted in the medical writings of Aetius Amidenus of Sebastea (modern Sivas, Turkey) that Saint Blase helped a woman whose son was choking and dying from a fish bone caught in his throat. According to legend, Saint Blase asked God to save this boy and miraculously, He did. Every year Catholics celebrate the Feast Day of Saint Blase on February 3rd and honor him with a ceremony that includes the '*Blessing of Throats.*' During this ceremony, the priest holds long white candles that are crisscrossed and bound together as he gently touches them to the worshipper's throat to bless them. Years ago, these candles were lighted, but several people got injured when their hair caught fire during the blessing. Candles are no longer lighted during the Saint Blase commemoration.

My third and dearest brother, was named after Saint Mark, the esteemed writer of the second Gospel. The Feast Day of Saint Mark is celebrated in the Spring, on

April 25 by both the Catholic and Eastern Orthodox Churches.

Growing up, Mark was especially fond of his middle name, Damian. Saint Damian had a twin brother named Cosmas and both of them are regarded by Catholics as the patron saints of physicians. They are occasionally depicted in paintings and books with medical emblems. Saint Anthony's Parish in Utica, New York, honors both Saints Damian and his twin Cosmas in an annual pilgrimage near their Feast Day which is September 27. Ironically, both of my brothers, Blase and Mark, like their namesakes, became doctors.

I was named after Saint Teresa of the Little Flower. Saint Teresa saw the world as God's garden, each person being a different flower, enhancing the variety and beauty in which Jesus delighted. Saint Teresa loved nature, and often used the imagery of nature to explain how God's Divine Presence is everywhere. Saint Teresa saw herself as "The Little Flower of Jesus" because she believed she was just like the simple wildflowers in forests and fields, unnoticed by the greater population, yet growing and giving glory to God. Because of this analogy, the title "Little Flower" remained with Saint Teresa. I liked that.

I had a statue of my patron Saint, Teresa of the Little Flower, which I kept next to my statue of the Blessed Mother on my dresser in my bedroom. I learned exactly what my patron saint looked like and wore from studying her statue. I also learned that she spelled her name without an "h" just like my name. This was important to me when I was a small child because I didn't want my patron saint confused with the other Saint Theresa who spelled her name with an "h." I always told people that I was named after Saint Teresa of the Little Flower and she did not spell her name with an "h." Apparently, there are a lot of Saint Theresas' out there.

As the youngest child and the only girl in my family, I was a bit of a brat, who pretty much got everything I wanted. I viewed Christmas as the best time of the year because I knew I would get a new doll along with all of my other presents. I loved dolls and enjoyed reading about them. I even learned how to make a doll out of corn husks from one of the books I checked out from the local library at Edmondson Village.

When I was just five years old, a nun at my first parish, St. Cecilia, gave me a nun doll. This nun (I can't remember her name) was a seamstress and made the clothes for my doll exactly like the clothes she herself wore. I had wondered what kind of hairdo the nuns had under their long black veil. I couldn't wait to take the veil off my nun doll to see the hairstyle. This was not easy, because under the veil there was a stiff white material which protruded out around the face of the doll just like the white head covering worn by a real nun. Once I got the stiff head covering off, I was shocked to see that the doll's head was completely bald.... shiny bald! I figured the nuns must love God a lot to shave their heads completely bald. I continued to investigate the doll's long black gown. She had a ropelike belt around her waist that had a miniature rosary attached to it. Beneath the gown was a long white linen slip covering white cotton underwear. Once I knew exactly what the nuns wore, I quickly redressed the doll so no one would know that I looked at her underwear or her shiny bald head. I still have this doll.

I had a lot of Catholic themed toys, even a toy altar about twelve inches tall, which I got at the Christmas Bazaar at St. William of York School. My toy altar had all the parts a real Catholic Church altar had, even a Tabernacle. The Tabernacle is a house-like structure where the sacred chalice containing the Eucharist is kept. The Eucharist is a round white wafer that we were taught becomes the Body of Christ when the priest blesses it. At Mass the priest gives the Eucharist to the people who come forward to receive Holy Communion.

The toy altar also came with a small gold colored chalice that I kept in the Tabernacle. I had a small boy doll dressed all in black. He was a bridegroom that I got with my bride doll for Christmas. I decided he would make a good priest and I could pretend he was saying Mass at my toy altar. Little did I know the fear and dread that a priest with a chalice would later instill in me.

I had my own holy water font on the doorway of my bedroom. A holy water font is a dish that holds water blessed by a priest. I blessed myself each day as I left my room with the holy water. I also had a large picture of Jesus with his heart in flames, that was blessed by a real priest. In the picture, Jesus' heart had thorns wrapped around it and fire coming out of the top. This picture frightened me when I was young. I believed everything I was told including that the priest was God on earth, and he was put on earth to help us in any way we needed.

Times were different in the 60's. Like most Catholics, the church was the center of our lives. No one ever questioned the priests or the nuns. Every neighborhood had a parish church and school where Catholics would go for just about everything… worship, education, guidance, social gatherings, etc.

The nuns taught me many things about the Roman Catholic faith, including that I should not play with kids who were not Catholic. I didn't understand why I shouldn't play with my neighborhood Protestant friends. When I asked the nun why, she told me that Protestants could not get into heaven so I should play with other Catholics with whom I would enjoy heaven when we died. This was my first experience with learned bigotry.

As Catholics we weren't supposed to eat meat on Friday so my mom usually fixed fish sticks for Friday dinner. We never questioned eating fish every Friday. As a matter of fact, I was told if you ate meat on Friday, it was a mortal sin unless you forgot; then it would be a venial sin. Venial sins were not as bad as mortal sins because you can burn them off in a place called Purgatory when you died. Purgatory was sort of a mini hell with fire and stuff. Once God feels as though you suffered enough in the fires of Purgatory you could get accepted into heaven. A mortal sin is different. If you died with a mortal sin on your soul which you committed by knowingly eating meat on Friday or skipping Mass on Sunday you would go straight to hell. No chance to get into Heaven.

Fortunately, there is a thing in the Roman Catholic Church called an *Indulgence.* An Indulgence is the remission of the temporal punishment for our sins. Merriam-Webster defines temporal punishment as follows:

*"A **punishment for sin** that according to <u>Roman Catholic doctrine</u> may be expiated in this world or if not sufficiently expiated here will be exacted in full in purgatory."*

Basically, an Indulgence erases some of your sins so you don't have as many to burn off in Purgatory. A friend of mine once told me how in an attempt to explain the way an Indulgence works, a nun drew a circle on the blackboard for her class and filled it in. Then she erased parts of the circle to show the class how Indulgences remove some of your sins. This process appears to save a lot of sinners. The Church says we can get these Indulgences because of the merits Jesus won for us by suffering on the cross. You can even get a Plenary or Full Indulgence for a loved one who died. So, if you love someone who died with a venial sin on their soul for like eating meat on Friday (by accident) back in the 60's and 70's you can make atonement for their punishment. With a Plenary Indulgence their soul can get out of the fires of Purgatory early and proceed to Heaven.

If you are seeking the Indulgence for yourself, you are asking for the pardoning of your sins while still alive so you won't have to suffer as long in Purgatory. The rules state that an Indulgence can be applied to oneself or to a deceased person, but not to other living people.

There is a list of things you need to do to get an Indulgence that mainly involves prayers and rejection of the desire to sin. You must be Baptized and be in the state of grace to accomplish this. This entire Indulgence thing was very confusing to me growing up. I wondered who created all of these rules and could I get to Heaven even if I missed Mass???

Then there is another place where people could end up when they die called Limbo. I was taught that Limbo was mainly for babies who were never Baptized Catholic. Since they were not Catholic but they really didn't commit sins per se, these babies would go to Limbo if they died. There were no fires in Limbo, which is a good thing, but the nuns told me that the babies in Limbo can never ever see the face of God. Apparently, our goal in life is to die, go to heaven and see the face of God. At least that is the way I understood things as a child.

Another rule I learned was that Catholics were not allowed to do any work on Sunday. Other Christian faiths also followed this rule based on the fourth Commandment, *"Remember the Sabbath day, to keep it holy."* The Jewish Sabbath is observed on Saturday, the seventh day of the week. For Catholics, Sunday was reserved as a day of prayer and reflection. Even the stores were closed on Sundays in the 1960's and early 1970's. To make sure merchants closed their stores, there was a thing called Blue Laws. Blue laws were also referred to as Sunday Laws because they restricted stores from being open on Sunday for religious purposes. Back when I was a child, we made sure we didn't need to buy anything important on Sunday. Like if you ran out of something necessary such as bread or toilet paper on Saturday you'd better get some right away because the stores wouldn't be open Sunday due to the Blue Laws. These laws were enforced in the United States as well as in some countries in Europe. They were slowly repealed with the sale of alcoholic beverages being one of the last remaining items that were forbidden to be sold on Sundays. Today, most young people don't even know what Blue Laws are. I'm glad we don't have them anymore.

As a young Catholic girl, I embraced my religion and I tried very hard to abide by all the rules even if I didn't understand them all. My religion was a source of peace because I knew how everything worked. I prayed to God by reciting the prayers I was taught in school. I believed I would go to Heaven because I was a "good" Catholic named after a holy saint. Later, I realized that the label "good" was also used to describe people who did things to hurt me and other kids, saying it was for our own good. What's in a name?

CHAPTER 3

SILENT SUNLIGHT

When all things were tall,
And our friends were small,
And the world was new.

I was born at Bon Secours Hospital in Baltimore, Maryland. My first home was on Monticello Road in Windsor Hills, a suburban neighborhood with rolling hills and large houses designed to accommodate the post-war Baby Boom. Though very young, I remember a little old lady who lived across the street from our house. She was so nice and even better, owned a long-haired black dog named *Happy.* I loved Happy with all my heart and played with him every day. One spring day the old lady knocked on our door looking for her dog. I was playing with Happy and giving him treats in our back yard. The lady watched me for a while then turned to my mom and told her that I could keep Happy as my very own dog! I was filled with delight and squealed with excitement, but Mom, not so much. She made a deal with the lady that Happy could visit me every day but had to go home at night.

When my mom told me, we were moving from Monticello Road to a new house, I was heartbroken. Not just about leaving Happy, but also about leaving my best friend, Tanya, and St. Cecilia Parish where my brothers went to elementary school. I liked St. Cecilia because they sponsored a cool Halloween parade every year. All the school kids dressed up like ghosts, goblins and even story book characters. They marched around the school for everyone to see. My favorite Halloween costume was the scary skeleton that my brother Mark wore. His mask had frightening glow-in-the-dark teeth with eye holes that looked like vast empty tunnels. Tanya went with me and my mom every time to watch the parade and cheer when we spotted the fanciest costumes. After the parade we gathered in the school auditorium for refreshments including tons of candy. I always had fun with Tanya who lived right next door. We would play games and draw in her playhouse. Tanya taught me how to draw beautiful tulips. I never forgot her.

But move we did, into a huge white colonial house with fancy black shutters on every window. It stood on the corner of Nottingham and Woodside Roads in Ten Hills, in southwest Baltimore. The front entrance had huge white columns on either side of the red brick porch. The upper floor had a spacious balcony on one side surrounded by four tall cedar trees and was accessible through French doors leading from the master bedroom. There was a smaller balcony on the other side of the house that was accessible through a large window in what would become my bedroom.

The homes in Ten Hills were built in the 1910's and ranged in style from English Tudor to Spanish Colonial to Georgian - - all with lots of detail. I loved the English Tudor houses. These had a classic old-world style of steep pitched rooflines with off-white stucco fronts accented by decorative dark wood. The Georgian houses were larger, square, brick homes characterized by lots of symmetrical windows with working shutters. The front entrance to these ornate Georgian homes was enhanced by arched entryways with tall columns on either side of wooden double doors. Ten Hills was popular for having these kinds of five and six-bedroom homes, lining shaded, winding roads and lush gardens with gorgeous flowering trees. It was a beautiful neighborhood.

I was five years old when we moved. Eager to explore this unfamiliar territory, I ran through my new house looking into all the rooms, reaching high on tiptoes trying out every light switch. Some of the light switches had two and three buttons which controlled ornate glass light fixtures hanging from the center of 12-foot-high ceilings. I opened and shut all of the interior wooden doors by turning the sparkling cut-glass doorknobs.

In my haste, I ran straight into my mom, nearly knocking both of us onto the old polished oak floor upstairs. "Slow down there, girl. Take a look at this..." Mom ushered me into my new bedroom. It had three windows! One window opened up to a balcony where I could see half way up Nottingham Road. I didn't realize then, how useful that high porch would be for me later. The spacious yard was surrounded by tall hedges, a sort of protective barrier between me and the outside world. I loved my new home. I felt safe there.

One evening, soon after we moved, I overheard my parents talking about the Ten Hills Swimming Club. The club had a brand-new pool and was just one block from our new house. I was so curious. I relentlessly asked questions about that pool. I wanted to see it. To get me out of her hair, my mom finally asked my big brother Joe to walk me down the hill to the pool, so I could see it for myself. We stood at the top of the parking lot adjacent to the pool. I could see a spacious brown club house with a high balcony porch next to the entrance. The pool itself was made of concrete painted sky-blue and shaped like an "L." There wasn't any water in the pool yet, but I could see two diving boards on the short leg of the "L." One diving board was pretty high above the pool and the other was much lower, but still too high for me. The number 12 was painted in black on the cement there. My brother told me the water would be 12 feet deep there once they filled the pool so people could safely use the diving boards. He explained that when you dive head first from a springboard, the water has to be deep enough so you don't hit the bottom of the pool too quickly and risk hurting your head or spine. I didn't think I would have to worry about that because the deep end of the pool looked too scary to me.

I turned my attention to the bottom of the pool on the longer part of the "L" which had darker blue stripes painted on it. Joe explained that these stripes were marking five swimming lanes which would be used for racing. I never saw anything like it before and couldn't wait for opening day.

My mom signed me up for swimming lessons on the first day the Hunting Hills Pool opened. She wanted to make sure I wouldn't drown. I soon learned all of the different swimming strokes. My favorite was the butterfly stroke where you lift both arms up at the same time lowering them ahead of you into the water while doing a dolphin kick with your legs. It's a powerful stroke. I swam it so fast I felt like I was going to fly right out of the water just like a real butterfly. Eventually I joined the swim team and won trophies and

SAFE IN SOCKS

ribbons swimming relay races doing the butterfly and back strokes.

I walked to the pool every day of every summer as a kid. There was a bulletin board next to the snack bar with announcements describing various events at the pool, scheduled throughout the summer. The dates and times for racing events were posted along with dates for Adult Only nights. Every Wednesday evening was reserved for adults, but it was the Saturday Teen Nights that caught my eye. There were pictures of kids having a great time at previous Teen Nights displayed on the bulletin board. I could see photos of teens dancing in the clubhouse and on the balcony overlooking the pool. Sometimes these gatherings had a theme, like a Hawaiian Luau. In the pictures I saw fancy tiki lights situated around the pool and party goers wearing beautiful Hawaiian lays made of tropical flowers. Several girls even wore grass skirts! Looking at the speakers, I could imagine music filling the air in and around the clubhouse. Sometimes there would even be a live band! The snack bar provided refreshments such as pizza, hot dogs, and soda.

The party wouldn't stop there. There were three wooden chairs towering over the pool that would be occupied by lifeguards who had a clear view of nighttime swimmers. At the first sign of twilight, the big circular underwater lights would turn on and the water took on a magical glow. Teen Night sounded like a dream to me and I couldn't wait to be old enough to go.

As a preteen, I often gazed out my open bedroom window on Teen Nights. I could hear music and laughing coming from the pool. Around 11:00, the music stopped and I watched the teenagers walk by my house as they headed home. They would pass right by my window filling the entire street, laughing and talking. I remember thinking it would take forever for me to turn 13, and I had a long time to wait before I could go to Teen Night.

The new house was only about four blocks from St. William of York Church and School, where my life continued to be inundated with Catholicism. My dad told me that when I had my own home, I should always live within walking distance from church because attending church is very important.

I enjoyed walking to school with some of my neighborhood Catholic friends. I never minded wearing the uniform at St. William's: a sleeveless navy-blue jumper with a diamond shaped patch inscribed with SWS for Saint William School on the front. White blouses with wide Peter Pan collars were worn underneath the jumper which allowed the collar to hang neatly over it. The boys wore navy-blue pants and white dress-shirts with a navy-blue clip-on tie. The uniforms were designed to make everyone feel equal. Nobody was dressed better than anyone else and I liked that.

Most classes at St William's were taught by nuns. Every nun certainly had her own quirks. My brother Mark, two years ahead of me at St. William's, told me that his teacher-nun always followed the boys into the bathroom during the restroom break after lunch. The nun would stand and watch the third-grade boys pee. This made my brother so uncomfortable that he never used the bathroom while in school. He actually developed a large bladder and to this day only needs to use the bathroom to pee once a day. Subsequently, other boys in my brother's class told me the same thing about the third-grade nun glaring at them when they went to the bathroom. Most of them did their best to try to hide themselves from the nun's prying eyes. What was up with that?

At St. William's, we were taught all the basic subjects: math, science, reading, history, English and geography, but religion was considered the most important. Much of the school day was devoted to religion. We said prayers in the morning, at lunchtime and before afternoon dismissal. In religion class, we were indoctrinated with the teachings, and principles of church law (known as *Canon Law*). There were no cannons anywhere and I have no idea why the church law was called that. I feared what would happen if I didn't obey all those rules.

Many church events were woven into our general studies. Often, we were lined up and marched to the church for activities like praying the Stations of the Cross on Fridays during the forty days of Lent leading up to Easter. Also, we were led into church for Confession before the first Friday of each month. Confessing our sins to the priest enabled us to receive Holy Communion at first Friday masses with a clean conscience.

Every Spring, we had a May Procession, a public display of faith. Much of the spring semester was dedicated to preparing for the procession in which the entire student body, first through eighth grades, marched around the school and the adjacent church building in their finest outfits. Second graders always wore their snow-white Holy Communion outfits to show off the fact that they recently received their First Communions. Every time, we gathered at the base of the statue of the Blessed Mother in front of the church. Here, one of the lucky eight grade girls, specially chosen to crown the white marble statue of Mary, would climb a ladder draped in white silk to place a beautiful crown of flowers on Mary's head. The chosen girl had the coveted honor of being that year's *May Queen*.

One year my family was chosen to make the sacred crown of flowers, a great honor. My mom had a beautiful garden that had many kinds of spring flowers. My brother Mark and I laid all the different types of flowers across the kitchen table. We carefully chose the prettiest flowers for our mom who wove them together into a perfect crown. I made sure my favorite - - lilies of the valley - - got included in the crown that year.

All the classes would gather in rows around the statue of Mary to sing songs of praise and joy as the *May Queen* carefully placed the crown of flowers on the head of the statue.

After this we continued the procession around the church and onto the playground, where we lined up to participate in the outdoor Benediction.

The Pastor was in charge of performing the Benediction, and a grand performance it was! The priest, dressed in colorful vestments, was always the central figure as he filled the role of God on earth before the adoring crowd. Robed altar boys catered to the priest's every need. The congregation sang out praises as he held up the Golden Sunburst Monstrance that encapsulated the holy host which was Jesus himself.

The priest would intone the "Divine Praises" (praises of God, Jesus, Mary, and the Saints) as the altar boys swung the medieval incense ball (censer) back and forth. The smell of frankincense was sent throughout the crowd, symbolizing the prayers of the faithful rising up to heaven. Yes, I believed all of this. Looking back, the props were amazing. Curious bystanders came from the surrounding neighborhoods to see this extravaganza. The fancily clad priest continually guaranteed a spectacular show much like a circus ringmaster charming the crowds. Parents proudly took pictures of their children as they sang in the procession. The May Procession was hours long, but a happy event.

As a child, here is what I learned about the Seven Sacraments of the Roman Catholic church.

Baptism: The priest pours water over your head when you are a baby to wash away Original Sin. He says some prayers while this is done and you are assigned godparents to witness this miracle. As I understood it, we are all born with original sin because Adam disobeyed God in the Garden of Eden when he ate the forbidden fruit Eve offered him.

Penance (now called Reconciliation): This is when you ask the priest to forgive your sins and hope he's not a pervert. After hearing your sins, the priest assigns you prayers to say, so God will forgive your wrongdoings.

Holy Communion (now called Holy Eucharist): You kneel before the priest to receive Christ in the form of a "host" made from unleavened bread. The nuns taught me not to ever let the holy host touch my teeth because to do so is a mortal sin, even if it touches your teeth accidently. Today, lay ministers are allowed to distribute Holy Communion and you can even accept the host with your hands, so I think it's ok if the holy host accidently touches your teeth now.

Confirmation: You are confirmed as soldiers of Christ around age twelve. A Bishop does the confirmation by reciting prayers. Then he slaps your face as he calls you by your chosen confirmation name. My parents insisted I pick "*Dolores*" as my confirmation name because it was my godmother's name. I didn't like that name and I felt left out when my friends got to choose any name they wanted as long as it was the name of a saint.

Extreme Unction or Last Rites (now called Anointing of The Sick): This is where the priest prays over and anoints the very sick or dying person. We were taught that sometimes God would heal the person being prayed over. Later in life when my dad was very ill and dying, I called St William's, where he had been a parishioner for forty-five years, to ask the priest there to come to my house to administer the Anointing of the Sick to my father. The priest said because I lived outside his parish (by about five miles) he could not come. I couldn't believe this and told the priest I thought my father wasted a lot of money at his fairy tale church. I ended up paying a local priest, Father Fell, about fifty dollars to administer the sacrament. I only did this because I knew it was important to my dad, who never lost his faith.

Holy Orders: This is when priests are ordained after completing Seminary training. They have to lie face down in front of the altar to take a vow of celibacy. A bishop anoints them with baby oil.

Matrimony (also called Marriage): In the Catholic Church, this is when a man and a woman form a covenant and promise to remain faithful to each other for the rest of their lives as husband and wife. We learned that the sanctity of marriage was serious, and the nuns warned us to be absolutely sure that the person you marry is someone you really want to live with for the rest of your life, because you would be stuck with them.

Out of all the sacraments, I liked Penance the least. In second grade, we had our first Confession. The priest waited on his side of a box shaped room called a confessional booth. I entered the other side of the booth which was separated from the priest's side by a screen-like panel. After saying a special prayer, I confessed my sins to the priest and asked for forgiveness. I was very nervous and eternally grateful that the priest couldn't see me through the screened panel when I went to confession as a child. Sadly, that would not be the case later on.

I was also afraid the first time I went to confession, because I didn't know what to say. I remember asking the nun what I should confess because I really didn't know what sins I had committed when I was seven years old. She asked me if I had brothers at home. I told her yes, I had three brothers. Sister asked if I ever argued with any of my brothers. I told her yes, we had arguments. Sister said, "Well, it's a sin to quarrel with your brothers and you need to confess that." Ok, I felt better that I had something to confess, but I had trouble pronouncing the word "quarrel" and I wasn't sure what it meant.

The priest absolves (forgives) you of all your sins after you confess them. You say an Act of Contrition, then exit the confessional to kneel in a church pew, to say the prayers the priest instructed you to pray. If you only committed venial sins, the priest usually assigned three Hail Mary's, two

Our Fathers and a Glory Be. I don't know what the priest tells you to say if you committed a mortal sin like killing somebody.

The nuns taught us to examine our conscience before confession, so we could figure out if our sins were mortal or venial sins (which I described in Chapter 2)

I learned more about hell in first and second grade. The nuns told me how I would burn forever and ever like a piece of charcoal, and even my mother couldn't give me one drop of water if I was bad and went to hell. Guilt and fear stayed with me.

All of the Church teachings were a part of who I was as a child. I really believed in the church and I tried to live up to righteous Catholic standards. I feared hell and felt guilty if I failed to abide by all of the rules I learned in elementary school.

Life Outside St. Williams

My mom constantly made sure I had fun things to do growing up. When I was around seven, she showed me books about tropical fish. After reading everything I could find about tropical fish, I became very interested in raising my own fish. One time, my mom surprised me and picked me up after school to take me to McCrory's, the local five and dime store. They sold aquariums and everything needed to set up a fish tank at home. It was there I picked out my first aquarium and some cool fish to put in it. Back then they didn't have separate pet stores dedicated to selling pets and supplies necessary for their care, like they do today.

Eventually, I learned how to set up larger thirty-gallon aquariums with efficient filtration systems to keep them clean. I started to breed some of the live-bearing fish like guppies, swordtails and mollies. It was much more difficult to breed the egg-laying fish. Soon I had several fish tanks in my club basement. Some fish could not live in the same aquarium because they didn't get along. For example, angel fish could not be in the guppy tank because they would eat all of the guppies. Also, guppy mothers ate their own babies so you had to separate the baby guppies from their mom as soon as she gave birth.

I enjoyed my hobby and even started a tropical fish club in my neighborhood. My friends and I would meet to talk about the different kinds of fish and trade them. I still keep tropical fish. I passed this hobby along to all of my children who also enjoy aquariums. Watching tropical fish is calming and can even lower blood pressure, which is why there are fish tanks in some hospital emergency rooms and doctor's offices.

McCrory also sold hamsters and guinea pigs. I spent a year or so raising both and giving them to my friends. I made cages in my back yard with chicken wire and spare wood from the garage, to give to my friends, along with their new pet. Unfortunately, some of the parents didn't share my enthusiasm for these small rodents, and they would send their kids back to return the pets. It was difficult for me to distinguish between male and female hamsters, and given their short gestation period of approximately 18-21 days, I soon became overwhelmed with them. Although the guinea pigs were easier to maintain and keep apart, my hobby turned into a major work project so I decided to seek out a more suitable pet. I ended up getting a beagle I called Yappy and he became my faithful companion.

I mentioned earlier how I looked forward to getting a new doll each Christmas. I usually got one on my birthday too, because I loved collecting dolls. My mom started getting me dolls the day I was born. Since I was the only girl, it seemed a fitting thing to do. This hobby has stayed with me. Currently my spare bedroom doubles as my doll room. I always thought I would pass my love of doll collecting down to my daughters or even to my future granddaughters. Sadly, none of my daughters or granddaughters got into dolls like I did. The grandkids won't even sleep in the spare bedroom because of "all the creepy dolls."

Ten Hills was a great place to explore on a bike. As I got older, I would spend my days biking all over the winding roads throughout our neighborhood. There were beautiful mature shade trees and flowering bushes in every yard. The houses along the roads were huge, designed to accommodate the large Catholic families who lived in them. It was common to meet people who were one of eight kids. One family on my street had ten kids. Another Catholic family along Edmondson Ave had eighteen kids! That was the largest family I knew of, that belonged to St. William's Parish.

We got a brand-new piano shortly after moving into our new house. I loved to listen to my mom play '*When Irish Eyes Are Smiling*' on our piano. I started to take piano lessons when I was around eight. I did pretty well and learned mostly popular songs. I still enjoy the piano and love to play along with my daughters during our Thanksgiving and Christmas get-togethers.

My mom also taught me how to bake. We had our own cherry tree in the backyard. In the Spring, my brother Mark and I often climbed the tree and picked bags of cherries for my mom's delicious cherry pies. Sometimes we had to fight off the birds who gathered, mostly in the morning, to grab their share of the delicious fruit. I became an expert at climbing that tree and was able to reach the biggest and brightest, red cherries at the very top. One year, my Mom baked over twenty cherry pies! She taught me how to make her perfect, light crust for the pies. It took me a while to get the hang of making the perfect crust. I learned that you didn't want to handle the mixture of flour, butter, and ice water too long because it would make the crust tough. Excessive mixing of the dough makes too much gluten develop, which causes toughness. I strived to make the perfect light tasting crust. My mom was a great teacher; she had the patience of Job.

Girl Scouts was a more structured activity I undertook. Girl Scout leaders consisted mainly of the moms of some of the scouts. We went on camping trips in Patapsco State Park. Certain activities earned badges for the sash that hung across the front of our uniforms. I earned my cooking badge first, then most of the Junior Scout badges. I progressed to the Cadette level before leaving the scouts to pursue basketball.

My dad hung an outdoor basketball hoop above our garage door making sure it was at the exact height used in professional basketball games. I spent hours playing basketball in our driveway after school. It wasn't long before some of my friends in the neighborhood joined in so we could play competitive games. Hours of playing and practicing paid off when I tried out for the St. William's Girls Basketball team. I made the cut and proudly joined the team. I loved the green uniform and got to choose number thirteen which I always considered lucky. I have many fond memories of playing basketball on that team.

It wasn't long before it was obvious that I needed braces. My teeth weren't really crooked but they protruded a bit so I ended up with, what other kids referred to, as train track braces. Metal bands were wrapped around my teeth and held together with a wire anchored to my back teeth which was used to pull my front teeth into place. I even wore an apparatus around my neck at night which hooked onto the wires in my mouth with rubber bands. This was designed to pull my teeth back. I was self-conscious about my braces for a while, but after I got use to them, I didn't mind it. My mom always told me to smile proudly because the braces showed that I cared about my teeth.

One of my biggest goals as a child was to become a lawyer like my dad. When I was very young, I used to carry his black leather briefcase around and pretend I was a lawyer. Sometimes I wore my bathrobe and sat behind the piano bench to make believe I was a judge. I lined up some of my dolls in my imaginary courtroom and called for order in the court by banging a crab mallet on the wooden lid of the bench. I was a dramatic kid.

My dad and I often watched the famous lawyer show, 'Perry Mason,' together on our old black and white TV. I was fascinated with legal cases and how they played out in court. One day I asked my dad if I could sue anybody. He replied, "You can sue anybody for anything, you just have to make it stick." I wasn't sure how to do that so I asked him to explain. I learned that you needed a precedent case, which is a case that has the same or similar set of facts as the case you were working on. The precedent case had already been ruled on or decided by the court and the court's decision in that case established law based on the facts. To convince the court to rule in your favor on your current case, you had to present a precedent case to support your argument. The Judge would read the precedent case to determine if the court's decision in that matter would match the decision you were pursuing in your current dispute. So, if you had the same basic facts in your case the Judge would usually rule in your favor if you introduced a similar precedent case to the court.

Judicial precedent is based on the Latin maxim: *stare decisis*. This means 'stand by what has been established and do not unsettle the established.' Adhering to these rules enables the courts to keep the law uniform. I hoped to be a judge one day.

Finally, after what seemed like forever, I got to go to my first Teen Night party at Hunting Hills Swimming Club. My girlfriend Margie met me at my house, so we could walk the one block down to the pool together. After we paid and got our hands stamped, we joined a group of young teenagers at the snack bar where we enjoyed pizza and soda. After eating, we walked up to the club house where the music was playing. I laughed and danced with my friends most of the night in the club house. We did take a break to swim, even though it was dark. The lifeguard could still see us in the water because the pool was fitted with underwater lights that illuminated the water. My first Teen Night was just as I imagined it would be. I was growing into a new phase of life. I was noticing boys.

CHAPTER 4

WILD FLOWER

I enjoyed most of my time at St. William's and learned a great deal while studying there. I was always good in math from first grade on and enjoyed the challenge it presented. My favorite teacher, Sister Joseph Francis, taught fourth grade where I learned public speaking. She instructed me to maintain eye contact during my oral reports in front of the class, which helped keep the audience's interest. Learning public speaking when I was young has been useful to me as an attorney. I developed a love for history in the fifth grade where my teacher, Mrs. Einstein, was passionate about our country's colonial days and made learning about that era very interesting. I loved to learn new things, which made elementary school pleasant.

However, the time I spent in the sixth grade at St. William's was weird. My class was assigned to an elderly nun, Sister Mary Daniel, who should not have had to teach pre-teens. The first couple of days were ok, but we had a group of incorrigible kids who literally took over our class. It was obvious from day one that this nun had no idea how to teach or maintain order. Kids talked non-stop and paid no attention to anything Sister said. Some of my classmates walked around the classroom joking and carrying on. One boy liked to stand at the front of the room pretending to be the teacher. Another boy and his buddy, threw a dodge ball back and forth nearly hitting the other students. A few daring girls drew pictures all over the blackboard, while others talked and giggled all day. It was a noisy room. Some of my classmates acted like Sister Mary Daniel wasn't even there.

On one occasion, one of the boys threatened to jump out the window and even stuck one leg out. The nun was traumatized as was I. This same boy slammed a basketball on the wooden floor with such force that it bounced back and hit the light on the ceiling, causing it to sway back and forth. Seeing this nun try to cope with the situation was stressful for those of us who just wanted to learn something. When it got really loud in the classroom, Sister would leave the room, stand outside the door, pathetically look through the window in the door and cry. This really bothered me and I never forgot her look of panic mixed with sorrow. Most of us were good kids who knew how to behave. Sister Paul Winifred, a no-nonsense nun who taught the other sixth grade class across the hall, would often come over to see what all the noise was about. She brought order to our class in no time. Nobody messed around with her.

Eventually, Mother Superior, who was short in stature, would arrive with her perpetual red face and stand at the front of the class glaring at us. Even the bad kids sat still when her beady eyes met theirs. Unfortunately, once order was restored, Sister Mary Daniel would have to come back in to teach the class. I could hear the poor woman plead with Mother Superior not to make her go back in. Sadly, Sister Mary Daniel had to do what she was told, even though it was obvious she couldn't pull it off. She tried everything. I remember one time Sister begged the class to behave, shouting, "What do you want to do?? Draw??? Here, draw!" She handed out art paper while trying to shout over the noisy students, "Here! Draw! Do whatever you want!" Once again, chaos reigned.

Finally, the pastor, Father Albert, came in and read us the riot act which scared everyone. You would think that would have ended the miserable situation. It did not. Why they didn't let that poor nun retire is beyond me.

Consequently, I got no sixth-grade education at St. William's. If any of my old classmates are out there, please contact me to tell me what your take on that school year was.

A ton of kids went to St. William's in the 60's and 70's. There were two classes, each with about three dozen kids, for everyday grade. Our class was known as 6.1, and across the hall, Sister Paul Winifred ruled over class 6.2.

The school finally took action to regain order over my class at the beginning of our 7th grade. When the new school year's class roster was handed out, I noticed that some of my friends were no longer in my class. The school decided to mix up the two classes, causing some old friendships to dissolve.

The idea was to separate the bad kids, mostly boys, so they could no longer gang up on the vulnerable older nuns.

The school also found one of the meanest nuns I had ever met to teach my seventh and eighth grade classes. I heard stories about this nun and how strict she was, but I figured since I was a good student, I didn't have anything to worry about. I could do strict, right? I mean, if it was for the greater good and enabled me to actually learn something in my last two years at St. William's, I felt I'd be ok. Wrong....

Sister Edna Maria was like no other nun or person for that matter, that I had ever met. What I learned from her was how to cope with evil mind games. I endured a great deal of torment from Sister Edna Maria in both the seventh and eighth grades at St. William's. One of the harshest punishments I received from her, was when she told me I would not be allowed to sing in the eighth-grade choir at the Christmas Pageant. I had dreamed about singing in that Christmas extravaganza since I first saw the eighth graders sing all the popular Christmas songs way back, when

I was in the first grade. Sister Edna Maria's reasoning for taking away my dream was as follows: Our class practised singing Christmas songs several times a week as December approached. On one occasion as I was singing along with my classmates, Sister Edna Maria started to walk up and down the aisles in the classroom. When she got to my seat she leaned way over and put her ear to my mouth. I was startled and sang very softly. She blurted out, "I can't hear you!" I tried to sing a bit louder to no avail, as she continued to lean into me saying she couldn't hear me. She got so close to me I could feel her stale breath on my face. Suddenly, she instructed the class to be silent so I could stand up and sing for all of them to hear. I was mortified. I was shy and I remained silent. She stretched this grilling ordeal out and kept demanding I sing. She went through the book of songs saying: "Well can you sing 'Oh Come all Ye Faithful'? How about 'Silent Night'?" She finally stopped and made a big announcement to my classmates: "Well since Miss Harris can't seem to sing, she will not be joining us at this year's Christmas Pageant." I was devastated. But I did not give her the satisfaction of seeing me cry. That day, I learned to not show my emotions.

Word of my being banned from the Christmas Pageant soon reached the other teachers. Most of the school knew that Sister Edna Maria could be very demanding, to put it mildly.

One really nice nun whom I had grown to love back in the fourth grade, Sister Joseph Francis, approached me after school to tell me she wasn't going to the Christmas Pageant either. When I asked her why, she said that the pageant fell on the same night that she had been scheduled to clean the convent basement. She asked me to join her because I was such a good worker. My good friend Mary Ann came over to say she would love to join us and help clean the convent basement. I knew Sister and Mary Ann were just being kind, but they made me feel so much better about this entire pageant thing. I was eternally grateful.

There were other incidents with Sister Edna Maria that, today, would be classified as child abuse. No teacher would ever get away with the continuing evil mind games I endured from that nasty nun.

One day, when she was handing out test papers to the class, she walked up and down the aisles putting passing grades face up on desks. She put the poorer grades face down. When she got to me, she shook her head and put my paper face down on my desk. I didn't believe I could have failed the test and, not wanting the others to think I failed, I turned it over to see a perfect score of 100%. Puzzled, I looked at Sister Edna Maria. She saw me. How dare I make eye contact! Sister grabbed my paper and stomped to her desk at the front of the classroom shouting: "Ok Harris, you think you're so smart!" She then spread books out over her desk – geography, math, religion, English, spelling... She yelled at me, "What do you think you deserve in these subjects? Well, what?!" I felt my face getting really hot. I had had enough. I looked her in the eyes and said: "A's, Sister, I deserve A's in all of them."

My voice was shaky when I said those words because until that moment, I had never stood up to this deranged woman who picked on me every day. I could hear some of my classmates making sounds of horror under their breath when I spoke out. Sister then blurted out questions from all of the books. I answered each one without hesitation. I was a nerd and I actually studied in grade school, so most of this came easy to me. Sister resorted to asking me where punctuation went in sentences, trying to trip me up. Even so, this day turned out to be my favorite experience with the bitch nun because I wouldn't let her break me.

Maybe other students have nice memories of this woman, but not me. She was a total bitch who tried to break my spirit and I stand by that. In hindsight, I think that perhaps in her own way Sister Edna Maria was trying to prepare me for things yet to come.

On to High School

I first heard about Keough when I was in the eighth grade at St. William's. My friends and I would talk about our upcoming graduation in the Spring of 1968 and which high school we hoped to attend. There was a brand-new high school for girls called Archbishop Keough. Adding to the excitement of potentially getting accepted to

Keough, was that our new 1968 incoming class would fill the school's capacity by completing the four grades for the first time. In 1967 Keough had freshmen, sophomores and juniors. When our class started as freshmen, the current juniors would become the first seniors to graduate from Keough. There would be 1200 students enrolled when filled to capacity.

I was intent on getting into Keough. There was an entrance exam and only about three-hundred places available in the freshmen class. The nuns at St. William's told us not to make Keough our only choice for our high school in case we didn't make the grade. We were reminded that eighth graders from all of the surrounding parishes would be taking that entrance exam. There was competition from St. Agnes, Our Lady of Victory, St. Bernardine, Our Lady of Good Counsel and other parishes I had not even heard of.

A comparable second choice was offered for us to consider - Archbishop Spalding High School, located in Severn, Maryland. Spalding was a new school too, founded in 1966. There was no way I wanted to go to Spaulding. It was much farther away, and at the time I didn't even know where Severn was. My heart was set on Keough.

Every day after taking the big entrance exam, I ran to the mailbox to check for my acceptance letter from Keough. I had heard from a few friends that they didn't get in, so I began to worry. I had been confident because I had straight A's, but I also understood that my score on the entrance exam would be considered along with my academic average when the school made their final decision. My only worry was about what my eighth-grade teacher, Sister Edna Maria, did to lower my average so I wouldn't achieve my dream. Sister could not give me anything under an A in all the subjects she taught me because I was that good. She knew all my grades would be averaged together, so she gave me a "D" in handwriting to bring down my final grade. This was bullshit! She purposely tried to undermine my application to Keough, my dream school. I was extremely upset and Edna delighted in it. This was not my imagination. My Mom made an appointment to meet with Edna after I showed her my report card with the "D" standing out from all the A's. I sat with my Mom at the nun's desk while she bravely presented our case showing Edna my papers with perfect Catholic cursive writing. Edna snapped back that my handwriting was subjective and looked like a "D" to her. My mom asked Edna to show her where my handwriting was so bad. Edna scrambled through my papers and pointed to a few spots where she thought some of my writing had gone under the line, again saying my penmanship looked like a "D" to her. My Mom could see how upset I was so she stood up and we left, only to go back the next day to appeal to Sister Edna Maria's soulless heart one more time. My mom asked Edna if she knew how much getting into Keough meant to me. No answer from her other than the results were the same, the "D" stood. I never understood why my dad didn't go to bat for me at that time. I do remember that the pastor, Father Albert, announced at Mass that he always stood on the side of the good sisters who taught our kids. I think my dad swallowed the *"Priest is always right!"* bullshit.

I made my mind up that I would ace the entrance exam and get into Keough, case closed. That is exactly what I did!

Even Sister Edna Maria's "D" in Handwriting didn't keep me out of Keough. I did not know then, how much I would later wish that Edna had given me "F's" across the board, to keep me out of Keough.

After being accepted, I went to the open house at Keough with my Mom. The tour was amazing. They had state-of-the-art language labs, science labs, art labs and even dark rooms for photography class. There was a sizable auditorium that would accommodate all the girls. We were told about Keough's Drama Club and how there was plenty of room in the auditorium for professional-quality school plays. I loved photography and drama and I couldn't wait to study both.

The guide continued the tour and led us to the gymnasium where the school's basketball team, the Keough Kougars, played against the other high school teams. The lower floor of the school had a huge cafeteria where all kinds of food would be available for the students. They even had a microwave oven for the girls to use. The countertop microwave oven had only become available to the public in the late 60's so having one in a school cafeteria was a big deal back then. You name it, they had it. Our escort was delighted to show us everything as she led us through the building. It was exciting to see the many opportunities Keough had to offer.

I remember when the guide showed us the chapel. She indicated Father Maskell's office was right next door and boasted that the girls had access to two priests at Keough. They could go to confession or talk over any problems they may have, or simply request guidance from either in this big new school. Priests were powerful figures within the Catholic Church and having two on call at Keough was amazing.

I remember feeling uneasy about sitting face to face with a priest to talk over problems and couldn't see myself ever doing that. When we had confession at St. William's, I always had that screened panel between me and the priest. The lights were very dim, so we really couldn't see each other. That made confession bearable.

CHAPTER 5

DARING ESCAPADES

I was beyond excited to be a freshman in high school. It seemed like a small city to me. I was a bit overwhelmed at first because everything was so much bigger than back at my familiar St. William's Elementary School. We were given green name tags and combination locks for our new lockers where we would be stowing our belongings. I soon found myself navigating hallways full of students also searching for their lockers. I clumsily shoved my things in my locker and joined the other freshmen for orientation in the spacious auditorium.

I entered Keough as a very serious and nerdy student and hoped to start my year off on the right foot. I was an honor student placed in advanced classes and bound for college. The campus setting was new to me and I was anxious to meet my new teachers.

We were instructed how to read our schedules, which were based on the modular system. The "mods" were periods of 20 minutes, which could be combined into periods of 40, 60 or 80 minutes for classes or independent study. This system made scheduling flexible so a class could vary in length, depending on the mods assigned to it. Instruction in language or science labs typically required longer periods, thus multiple "mods." We were assigned one or two open mods to be used for study time, meeting with teachers or eating lunch. It was an adaptable system. I was happy at Keough and I wanted to learn. I dreamed of being a doctor or an attorney like my dad.

I joined all the clubs I could get into when I started ninth grade. I enjoyed public speaking and drama. But, lots of students were trying out for the Drama Club. Apparently, many of the other girls wanted to be actresses like me. So, sadly, I didn't make the cut. I'm glad I tried out, though, because this was how I met Sister Cathy, who taught English and drama. I could never have imagined then, the part Sister Cathy would play in the rest of my life.

My interest in drama continued throughout my freshman year. I tried out for a part in a musical, Li'l Abner, a story about a poor mountain village called Dogpatch. Try-outs were held at Mount Saint Joseph High School, a nearby school for boys, staffed by the Xaverian Brothers. My dad and all of my brothers went there. I had heard stories about how some of the Brothers were extremely strict and even hit students if they got out of line. Nevertheless, I went there after school with my friends to try out for a part in the play. I sang "*I Get by With a Little Help from My Friends*," and was cast in the chorus, which sounded good to me. We were told to make our own costumes to look like ragged dresses worn by the poverty-stricken mountain people of Dogpatch.

Participating in this play was great fun for me, especially the part about the Sadie Hawkins Day Race. That was the one day out of the year that a mountain girl could catch a boy for the purpose of marriage. Of course, the boy would run like crazy to escape this fate. During this scene I joined the other girls and chased the terrified boys all around the stage, jumping over the elaborately re-created bushes and fences of Dogpatch. I zeroed in on one of the cute St. Joe boys, tackled him and proudly held him down with my foot, thereby claiming him as mine. The audience roared with laughter at the sight of the girls showing off their apprehended fellas.

Recently, in a fortunate stroke of serendipity, I have reconnected with one of the girls from the chorus of Li'l Abner who was a year ahead of me back at St. William's. Anne not only shared her fond memories of the play, she showed me her saved Li'l Abner brochure that listed the entire cast. Anne further revealed to me that she, too, was a survivor of childhood sexual abuse and that she recognized me from watching *The Keepers*. It is delightful to have Anne back in my life, to fondly reminisce about our days back in elementary school, and laugh at how far we have come.

It was not all fun and games starting out as a freshman, however, and fitting in with the other girls became a struggle for me. I soon learned that there were closed groups called cliques at Keough just as at other large high schools. The girls belonging to these tight networks rarely hung out with, or spoke to those outside the group. Usually, a popular girl would take a leadership role within the group and the others would act as her "followers." I was never welcomed in any of the popular cliques at Keough. Sometimes other students would avoid me because I was such a serious student and lacked confidence with regard to my social skills. I was definitely a nerd, but I wanted to blend in with the others. I longed to belong, to socialize.

I had a lot of body image issues when I entered high school, which contributed to my low self-esteem. This didn't help my situation or my feeling of being left out. Gym class was a huge struggle for me. In gym class, the girls would change into their athletic clothes right in front of their lockers. I was so self-conscious about my body that I hid in a shower stall to change into my gym uniform. I felt that my boobs were too small or weird or different and I certainly did not want anyone to see me undressed. I feared being made fun of. Some of the popular girls could be very cruel. I often witnessed them mocking and teasing other new students who were just trying to get through the day.

Lunch was not as bad. My lunch table was made up of girls I had known at St. William's, as well as a few new girls I met who were easy-going and not trying to be in charge. I found that in high school, there were basically three groups of young adults.... greasers, nerds and hippies.

Greasers tried to act rebellious by wearing black leather and driving fast cars or motorcycles. Greaser boys wore their hair greased-back with wax or hair gel which is where the term "greaser" came from. They would usually wear black leather boots or loafers with white socks. The greaser girls typically wore their hair teased high and sprayed into place. I did not like the look of, or the loud way these girls talked about their dates and other social activities.

The nerdlike individual was typically intellectual and somewhat of an obsessive introvert. Social skills were lacking, which made it difficult for them to connect with others. Nerds never worried about being alone or even combing their hair. They focused on solving problems and just getting where they were scheduled to be. I had fallen into this category, not by my own choosing, but because I spent most of my time focusing on my grades and getting from point A to point B. I was awkward, content to read, study and learn; thus, not much of a conversationalist. One time I was alone quietly eating lunch at Keough, when another freshman approached me to say hello. I looked up smiling, but my grilled cheese sandwich somehow started to get all over my hands and face. Suddenly, I had forgotten how to eat. Throwing caution to the wind, I introduced myself in a way to put myself right out there as the dork I thought I was. "Hi, my name is Teresa and I'm a spaz." This freshman, a girl named Vonnie, burst into laughter as she sat down to join me saying, "Ok Teresa the spaz, nice to meet you." We remain friends to this day.

The hippie-types, sometimes called "heads", were very accepting and friendly. The term "heads" referred to a desire to gain knowledge or to give your brain something to "feed" on. It could also mean to experiment with drugs, mainly hallucinogens, such as LSD. The band, the Jefferson Starship, explained this late 1960's phenomenon in their popular song "White Rabbit". The lyrics instruct the listener to "feed your head," much like the white rabbit in Alice in Wonderland encourages Alice to try something new. If you want to "follow the white rabbit," you are open to trying new things and exploring the unknown, potentially dangerous world of drug use. Some hippies saw LSD as a means to expand their knowledge greatly, and live outside the hard rules followed by the "Establishment." These individuals were often referred to as "heads."

Generally, hippies didn't seem to judge people. Most rejected the establishment and supported civil rights. Both male and female hippies typically wore their hair long, straight and parted in the middle. Fringed jackets and love beads accented their wardrobe. Hippies developed their own music scenes gravitating towards artists who had something to say, such as Bob Dylan, Joan Baez and the group Crosby, Stills, Nash and Young. The Woodstock Music Festival in 1969 put the Hippie Movement in the public eye. I saw myself as more of an average hippie, full of peace and love, not a hardcore "head." I bought myself a purple suede fringed jacket, changed my name from Teresa to Terry and developed a new way of expressing myself.

1969.... The Summer of Love.

In the late 60's, Vietnam was pictured in the news daily, marches to end the war and to promote equal rights for African Americans and women were happening in nearby Washington DC. I made new peace-loving friends and we all looked like hippies. I spent my free time listening to music, wearing flowers in my hair and love beads around my neck. I completely remade myself and started hanging around Ellicott City, Catonsville and Columbia, where groups of young people gathered. I loved going to Lake Kittamaqundi in Columbia, Maryland, which had become a haven for guitar-playing, long-haired hippie-types.

At age fourteen, I was allowed to go out with boys if it was a group date. My parents believed in strength in numbers, meaning I would be less likely to get physical with a guy if a crowd were present. I had been to dances with my friends, Teen Nights at Hunting Hills Pool, CYO events at St. William's and other parishes, all with parent chaperones. They were there to make sure we did not dance too close and that no funny business took place. But

I really wanted to date a boy without a group watching everything I did.

When I was almost 16, I met a guy named Josiah at the lake front in Columbia. We talked about everything from Woodstock to the infamous Catonsville Nine, a group of conscientious objectors to the Vietnam War. The "Nine" charged into the local draft board, stole the draft cards, poured homemade napalm over them and set them ablaze. Their actions of protest against both the draft and the war in Vietnam, filled the airways and newspapers. Lots of young people, including Josiah, were against war and opposed the mandatory draft. This issue was close to my heart, because my three older brothers were old enough to get drafted and I didn't want them to get butchered in the jungles of Vietnam. America was in a time of unrest. The slogan, America, Fix it or Fuck it, became sort of a battle cry for the peace-loving hippie generation.

Josiah and I exchanged phone numbers and soon became inseparable. We did everything together and saw each other as often as possible. I could visit him at his house as long as a parent was home. I usually got a ride to his house in Catonsville from one of my older brothers. Josiah would greet me at his front door, and we would retreat to his music room where we could listen to albums and talk. On most weekends his friends would stop by. He was in a band and I often stayed to watch him practise with his friends.

Not long after we met, both of us got our driver's licenses which gave us even more freedom. He was my first love and I couldn't have been happier.

Coffee Houses

Back in the 60's and 70's a "coffee house" was a social event. The name was derived from the main beverage served at these non-alcoholic gatherings. Juice, tea and desserts were typically available as well. These encounters were often held to raise awareness of social causes such as equal rights. Josiah and I would often go to local coffee house events. These get-togethers were a welcoming place for meeting people who shared similar ideas about life. You could find coffee house events at nearby high schools, colleges, or church halls. They were different than school dances -- more intimate. You usually sat around tables drinking coffee, eating small snacks, and talking while listening to folk-rock music from aspiring musicians. I loved listening to songs of protest and activism. Bob Dylan's "The Times They Are A-Changing", is still one of my favorites. The atmosphere of a coffee house filled the room with a kind of shared humanity. I liked that.

The coffee houses could get a bit wild at times. One time, my good friend Linda and I went to a coffee house at Cardinal Gibbons, an all-boys' Catholic High School a mere football field away from Keough. As we arrived, I could see teens smoking pot in a nearby wooded area. Linda and I joined them and drank from a communal bottle of Boone's Farm Strawberry Hill wine that was being passed around. I liked the sweet taste and drank a bit more. Slightly tipsy, we went into the coffee house.

Once inside, Linda and I found an empty table and sat down. I was feeling uneasy. A feeling of panic overwhelmed me. I turned to Linda and asked her if she was okay. Linda said yes, she was alright, but she did not look okay. About a half hour later, I started to see things. I could see printed music scores floating by my head. The music came directly out of the notes that were printed on the scores. I saw baby birds bursting with color circling around our table. I looked at Linda. It looked like she was trying to say something, but she seemed to be sitting a million miles away at the other end of the table. The table appeared to be shrinking and stretching and shrinking again. I could hear people laughing and joking telling us, "You got tabbed." This was supposed to be a good thing, a gift. Unknown to me, someone had put several "tabs of acid" in that bottle of wine we drank. I quickly learned that acid or LSD was a hallucinogen and it makes you see and hear things that aren't really there. Now, I liked to have a good time and I had enjoyed wine and a little pot now and then in the past, but LSD??? No way, too weird. I never liked it.

That night I was staying at Linda's house. After the coffee house ended, we managed to walk out to the parking lot to meet her dad who was picking us up. We jumped into his car laughing and giggling, after he pulled up to where we were standing. Afraid that he would know we were high, we both shut up and remained silent during most of the ride home. A few times Linda's dad started talking and all I could hear were strange noises coming from my purse which was lying across my lap and beginning to melt. My purse started to feel incredibly hot and heavy, like a molten rock. It started to look like it was dripping onto the car seat. I struggled to push it to the floor. Thankfully, Linda seemed to have the situation under control as she told her dad how wonderful the band at the coffee house had been. Her dad played the trumpet in a band and I thought it was great Linda was talking to her dad, since I could not form words. I just kept quiet until we reached her house. Once there, Linda and I ran up the steps leading to her bedroom shouting thank you and good night behind us to her parents. Fortunately, we didn't need to interact with them that night. We were tripping. We desperately needed sleep.

CHAPTER 6

"LET'S GO CRAZY" by PRINCE

Chapter 6 is divided into seventeen parts by subtitles, each of which details how Maskell's sexual games destroyed the once curious, content girl inside me. My mind was altered forever. At times I believed I was totally insane. I became a different person and had difficulty trusting anyone. But as time went by, I adapted to a new version of me. Ultimately, I was determined to survive no matter what he made me do.

"TERRY HARRIS, PLEASE REPORT TO FATHER MASKELL'S OFFICE..."

Mom noticed a change in my behavior. I had been experimenting with wine and weed while out partying with my newfound friends. I had changed my wardrobe to create a new hippie-like appearance. I guess my personality had changed a bit. I felt like I was less of an introvert; I was much more outgoing. Mom and I were always very close, but I no longer felt like sharing everything with her. I was trying to find myself and I wasn't sure what I was looking for. I kept my relationship with my boyfriend to myself, sharing the bare minimum, only telling her where we were going. I guess you could say I was acting mysteriously. All of this led to that horrible day when my mom found that weed and paraphernalia in my purse. If only I could have been more careful that day. If only...

The 'searching of my purse' incident ultimately led to my sexual abuse by Father Maskell and later by his friends. I have decided to share some of what happened to me while I was under Maskell's control, in his office at Keough, in the chapel adjacent to his office, in his private bathroom in his office, in his car during police runs and in his private living quarters at St. Clement's rectory in Lansdowne, Maryland.

I was forced to have sex with several of Maskell's police friends and repeatedly probed by his gynecologist buddy, Dr. Christian Richter. I was sent to a psychiatrist, Dr. Guzman, because Maskell "diagnosed" me as being a schizophrenic. I was subjected to hours of bizarre mental testing by both Father Maskell and the school psychologist, Dr. William Urban.

After a few sessions with Maskell, I did seek help from the other priest who provided counseling at Keough, Father Neil Magnus. Magnus had an office on the second floor of the school. I knocked on his door and as he opened it, I asked him if he could take over my counseling session that Maskell had started. Magnus turned me around and lead me out the door as he said he couldn't help me. I later learned from my attorneys in my 1995 Doe/Roe case that Magnus had his own sex ring operating at Keough and even participated with Maskell abusing girls.

ESTABLISHING A ROUTINE

After my initial meeting with Maskell I had to report to him whenever he called me out of class. I would be in class and a voice would come over the intercom instructing me to report to Father Maskell's office, or to the school nurse's office, where he would meet me. This happened three to four times a week in the beginning.

I was trapped. Maskell had convinced my parents that he was there to save me. He was to be my guide and my confidante. He told them he would be available all hours of the day or night, just to help me. My dad thought I was extremely lucky to have such a kind and important priest right there at Keough who was willing to help me through my teenage years of confusion. A priest who was willing to help me reconnect with my parents, to recreate the loving bond we once had. This to them was truly a gift from God.

I didn't know back then what the term *"grooming"* meant, but since then I have come to realize that Maskell was a master groomer. I have learned from professionals such as psychiatrists and psychologists as well as from other survivors and their families that *grooming* is the act of building a relationship of trust and emotional connection with someone so they can manipulate, abuse and exploit them. Young people who are groomed can then easily be sexually abused or exploited. This process can be achieved over a short period of time, in just a matter of weeks. As a master groomer, Maskell built a relationship with my parents to make himself appear trustworthy and authoritative. He used his knowledge of psychology to persuade my parents that only he could save me from the destructive path I was on, one that was sure to lead to a life of reckless, wild behavior. His manipulation didn't stop there and as time went on Maskell used his *grooming* talent on me. He made me totally dependent on him as an important link between myself and my parents. There were days when he attempted to convince me that he cared deeply about me and only wanted what was best for me. He repeatedly told me he loved me very much. With his skills and the use of *Thorazine* and God knows what other kinds of drugs, he even controlled my very thoughts.

NO END IN SIGHT

Several days after my first encounter with Maskell. I was sitting in my classroom when suddenly the intercom startled me. "Terry Harris, please report to Father Maskell's office." All eyes on me, I painstakingly rose to leave the classroom. I could feel my heart pounding in my throat. My mind was racing. "What could he want now?" I thought. Not knowing what to expect, I trudged down the long hall leading to Maskell's office. His door was open. I could see him sitting in his throne-like chair at his intimidating wooden desk. He looked up, saw me, and rose to greet me at the door. He led me inside his office and locked the heavy door behind us. I knew then that something bad was going to happen.

Once inside, Maskell pulled his mammoth chair around to the front of his desk. He told me to kick off my shoes. He leaned into me and started to unbutton my blouse. He slipped off my blouse and pulled my undershirt up over my head. He stared at my bare breasts and began fondling them. He unzipped my skirt. As before, he let it drop to the floor. And then my underpants. I held my head down and stared at my socks, thankful that I got to keep them on. He unbuckled his belt and unzipped his fly. He pulled me roughly onto his hard penis and we fell into his chair.

I gagged. I thought I was going to vomit. I could smell his sweat as he touched every part of me. His breath was hot against my neck. He hurt me terribly as he raped me. When he was done, he threw me onto the cold hard floor, where I just sat in pain and fear for a long time. I don't even know how much time passed before I found the courage to look up. I saw him shuffling papers on the other side of his desk. He glanced at me and handed me a drink in a paper cup. Then he reached into one of the desk drawers and pulled out a cigarette to offer me. My hand trembled as I grabbed the cigarette much like a hungry dog would snatch a bone. He tossed me a pack of matches and I managed to use them to light my smoke. I remained in his office until the end of the school day, too terrified to speak. No matter how hard I tried, I couldn't remember how I got dressed. Next thing I knew, he drove me home and let me out of his car. I ran into my house, managing to smile slightly at my mom as I darted upstairs to get to my room.

DON'T TALK ABOUT IT

Several days after that encounter with Maskell, I sat in class trying to listen to my math teacher, Mr. Ball. He was a friendly teacher and I didn't mind his class at all. I always liked Math. I was placed in an advanced algebra class when

I first entered Keough as a freshman. The intercom above the classroom door came on again, breaking my focus on solving linear equations. This time the voice announced, "Terry Harris, please report to the nurse." Racing thoughts flooded my mind. I didn't feel sick, why do I have to see the school nurse? My classmates were silent as I got up to leave. I could see how many students were blissfully unaware of the things going on behind Maskell's closed door. Not knowing what to expect, I tentatively entered the health suite. Mrs. Stafford, one of the school nurses looked up from her desk to say, "Father Maskell wants to see you. Here's a hall pass." Wondering why I wasn't just called directly to his office, I walked with trepidation down the hallway... to insanity.

As before, the door was open, Maskell was sitting behind his desk. He gestured for me to come in, not even bothering to get up. This time, soft music played from a radio on a small table next to him. The music was interrupted by a station announcement stating that we were listening to WLIF, Life radio.

Maskell got up from his chair and walked toward me. When he suddenly embraced me, I let out a soft cry. He locked the door and told me that he only wanted what was best for me. He pulled the chair around to the front of his desk, sat down and again pulled me into his lap. He talked about how he was not supposed to touch the girls that came to him for guidance. He added that he found touching the girls and holding them was the best way he could help. He told me about his boat, and how he would take troubled girls out sailing. Some of the girls, he claimed, made up terrible lies about him, that he made them do bad things on his boat. He cupped my face in his hands so that my eyes looked directly into his. He asked me if I would say bad things about him. I froze. I felt his huge hands remove my blazer as he was talking, saying he had to get rid of his boat because of those evil girls. He paused, still glaring at me. "You would never tell anyone that I did bad things to *you*, Terry, would you?" I whispered, "No Father, never." He pulled me closer, pushing my head into his lap and onto his exposed penis. He was demanding that I perform oral sex on him. I became nauseous; I felt like I was going to throw up. I pretended to myself that I was in a warped bizarre episode of the *Twilight Zone.*

Maskell's mood shifted abruptly. He growled harshly that if I ever did say anything about a priest, nobody would believe me, a druggy. He held my head tightly in his hands again, uttering menacingly that he could hurt me badly, and that no one would care. Suddenly, Maskell drew a gun from his desk drawer and laid it down on the desk. He bragged that he was an excellent marksman. Still naked and trembling, I assured him that I would never ever tell anyone anything, and certainly not bad things about him.

He ordered me to get dressed. He then told me I could stand outside and smoke a cigarette behind the white cement grid located in front of his back door. The wind felt cold against my face and my feelings of nausea slowly dissipated. Although Maskell told me I could return to class, I headed for the cafeteria instead, in an attempt to find a place where I could calm down.

THE GYNECOLOGIST (The Not-So-Christian, Christian)

As I sat lost in thought in my English class, the familiar voice came over the public address system once again, instructing me to report to Father Maskell's office. I felt physically ill as I ventured slowly down the long hallway. This time, the door was partly ajar. I tapped it and it opened wide. Maskell was putting on his overcoat and told me he was taking me to a doctor. He said he had informed my dad that I was sexually active and that I should be examined for possible venereal diseases. Maskell told me that my dad had thanked him and had given him permission to take me to a gynecologist and bring me home afterwards.

We drove into Baltimore to the Medical Arts offices on Read Street. Once there, a nurse took me into a small room and told me to take my clothes off. She instructed me to get up onto the examination table; then she left. Maskell entered the room. He directed me to recline on the hard metal table and he put my feet into the stirrups. At the time I didn't know what stirrups were or how to place my feet on them.

Once I was situated on the exam table, Maskell's friend, Doctor Christian Richter, came into the room. He began to examine my breasts. Maskell positioned himself between my feet at the end of the table. He pushed down hard on my stomach; it hurt so bad. He said he just needed to make sure everything was okay as he inserted some kind of medical device and painfully stretched my vagina. He then removed the device and leaned into me slowly inserting his penis into my vagina. I was numb. I stared at the ceiling. I stared at my blue wool knee-high socks and imagined I was someplace else. I wasn't even in my body. I was a spectator watching another girl in a horror movie.

When Richter and Maskell finished with me, I mindlessly got dressed and followed Maskell back to his car. He was cheerful, satisfied and hungry. He asked me if I had ever eaten a meatball sub. I told him I didn't eat subs. Nevertheless, he told me that we were going to a pharmacy to pick up some items that Doctor Richter said I needed and then we would get submarine sandwiches to eat at his rectory home. He guaranteed that I would absolutely love a meatball sub.

We arrived at a small drug store near St. Clement's Church, where Maskell resided in the rectory. We entered the drug store and Maskell led me down the feminine hygiene aisle where he picked up a hot water bottle that had a long hose with various attachments. Next, he grabbed a big jar of Massengil douche powder that appeared to have a pale yellowish color. I was puzzled. Maskell explained to me that the hot water bottle was for douches and enemas and now I could use it to keep myself clean. He told me I needed a douche every day to stay healthy. Picking up a bottle of feminine deodorant spray (FDS), he told me it was to keep my private area smelling nice. He commented gleefully that he liked to spray his balls with the FDS because it made him feel so fresh. The look of horror on my face made him laugh. He wanted to know if I was embarrassed shopping for feminine things with a priest. I began to feel nauseous. Walking to the rear of the store, Maskell greeted the pharmacist, saying that he had "another one from Keough" (meaning me.) They both peered down at me. The priest added that you could tell I was an upperclassman, a junior, because I wore blue knee-high socks. He added that freshmen and sophomores wore gray knee-high socks, explaining that it was a rite of passage to switch over to blue knee-highs when you became a junior at Keough. The pharmacist smiled at me as Maskell handed him several of my prescriptions that Dr. Richter had written for my vaginal irritation.

It wasn't until years later that I learned what some of the medications I had been prescribed back then were for. I recently showed my good friend Anne Copeland several letters between Maskell and Richter that I had saved from my days at Keough. Anne had attended St. William's grammar school with me and I reconnected with her after *The Keepers* aired. One of those old letters stated that I had vulvitis (vaginal irritation) for which Koromex Douche was prescribed. Anne worked as a pharmacist for many years and she informed me that Koromex is the 9-nonoxynol that is the spermicide used in condoms. It has nothing to do with vaginal itching/irritation or vulvitis. It is purely a spermicide, a contraceptive, and if used immediately before or after coitus, it might help to prevent pregnancy. Why would Maskell be purchasing this stuff for me back then?

Strangely, back at the pharmacy, when Maskell got out his money clip to pay for everything, I actually felt guilty that he was spending his money on me. Where does a priest get his money? Was this part of his salary for saying Mass and hearing confessions? I wondered.

Next, we pulled up to a small carry-out sandwich place. I walked with Maskell up to the counter where he ordered two meatball subs, "With the works." He instructed me to grab two cokes from a nearby refrigerator. Again, I felt guilty when he got his money clip out to pay the cashier for our food.

We pulled up to the rectory at St. Clements in Maskell's spacious pale blue car which had filled with an appetizing aroma from the bag containing our warm subs. It was dusk and I knew my mom would be fixing dinner at home. I yearned to be with her, helping her set our dinner table instead of being with Maskell. I walked in the front door of the rectory with Maskell who was carrying our food and the pharmacy bag. A woman was sitting at a table just inside the kitchen. Maskell introduced her as the housekeeper, Mrs. Whatever. I felt so apprehensive, I forgot her name as soon as he said it. We proceeded right past her and climbed the stairs leading to his room, which was in the front of the building over the front door. I noticed the floor in the rectory appeared all uneven and shifted weirdly when we walked on it. Once we reached Maskell's room, he directed me to sit on his couch, which was covered in a dark fabric. He emptied the pharmacy bag and laid out all the items neatly on the coffee table in front of the couch. Next, he set out our dinner, complete with white linen napkins he got from a drawer in his stereo cabinet. I must have been hungry because, strangely, I never tasted anything as good as that meatball sub.

Maskell turned on some Irish music and disappeared into another room. A short while later he called me into his bathroom and demonstrated how he cleaned his toilet, stressing the importance of a clean toilet. His toilet had an open black seat like those you see in public bathrooms. The hot water bottle was now in the sink and he was filling it with water. He added the Massengill powder and shook it up. Coming from the top of the bottle was a long hose where you screw on the lid. On the end of the tube was a circular attachment with holes in it, like a sprayer used for washing hair. He told me to take my skirt and underpants off and to sit on the black toilet seat. I was mortified. With one hand, he spread me open and with the other, pushed the white attachment on the end of the tube into my vagina. He hung the bottle on a hook that was on the back of the door so gravity would force the water out through the holes in the attachment to clean me inside. I never had a douche before. Christ, I didn't even know what a douche *was* until then. Maskell told me he would take everything to his office at Keough so I could take douches every day. I felt dizzy at that point and again as before, only remember getting out of his car to walk up the front steps of my house.

At subsequent visits to the gynecologist, Maskell would always stay in the examination room, saying he was there to assist the doctor. He claimed he had also studied to be a physician, but that God called him to do His greater work as a priest. During one exam, Maskell pushed my legs apart and stuck his fingers inside me. He laughed as he said he could fit a freight train in my vagina because it was so big. It was around that time that I began having thoughts of suicide.

"THE SOUNDS OF SILENCE" by Simon and Garfunkel

Back at school the following day, I was called out of my early homeroom class to report to Father Maskell's office. When I entered the office, he was in an angry mood and reminded me that he had a gun. He told me that if I shared what was going on with anyone, he would kill me and kill my family too. He added that he could easily have me placed in a "school for bad girls," that he called Montrose, if I made up lies about him. He said it would take only one brief phone call from him and I would be sent there immediately. He said that nasty delinquent girls were sent there and that they would not hesitate to beat me up. Then, Maskell held my head in his hands and tearfully told me they didn't serve whole hotdogs at Montrose and that I should know why. I looked puzzled. He started to sob as he told me that the girls at Montrose shoved anything they could get their hands on up their vaginas, and since hot dogs resembled penises, the staff there always served them cut up. He said the girls at Montrose were wicked and would hold me down and stuff things into my vagina, maybe even sharp things that would make me bleed. I was terrified. I didn't know what would be worse, being sent to Montrose or being shot with the gun he liked to brandish.

Maskell's mood quickly changed and he embraced me. He told me he loved me as a father loves a daughter. He pulled me onto his lap and told me how if he were my father, he would raise me to be a good girl, a girl who was pure, and virtuous. He started to gently rock me back and forth and asked me if I believed in God. For some reason I said no because if there was a God, I wouldn't have to be with him. Surprisingly, he didn't get angry, but instead started talking about all of the magnificent things in nature and how only a divine being could create such beauty. He said he only wanted what was best for me and to teach me about the wonders all around us. I sipped a Coke he had given me and drifted off to sleep right there in his lap.

Next thing I remember was the chill in the air as I got into Maskell's car. He drove me home and walked with me up to my front door. My dad greeted him as I walked swiftly past them so I could flee to my bedroom.

"WITH A LITTLE HELP FROM MY FRIENDS" by The Beatles

In my junior year, I had a small circle of trusted friends at Keough. We all sat at the same table in the school cafeteria every day for lunch. It wasn't hard for my buddies to figure out that something was very wrong with me. I told my closest friends about what happened at home that had led to me having to see Maskell all the time. Fearing the priest, I told them only a little bit about what went on in his office. I made sure they all knew he was a pervert who liked to act out very weird fantasies. I was open about having to take douches and the visits to the gynecologist accompanied by Maskell each time. I was never sure if they ever figured out that Maskell himself administered the douches to me in his bathroom. Linda knew, she watched him do it several times when we reported to his office together.

Most of my friends and I were already sexually active with our boyfriends. We certainly were not ignorant about sex. After all, it was the late 60s. But what was happening to me.... not just physically but emotionally and mentally in Joseph Maskell's office...... was not normal by a long shot.

One cold winter morning, Maskell again called me to his office. I had just arrived at my homeroom class for attendance and morning announcements. I was running late at home that morning and inadvertently put on a pair of old socks with holes in them. I realized this after Maskell informed me that we were going to see Dr. Richter again, later that day. I knew Maskell would make fun of my holey holy socks! I knew I would be allowed to keep my socks on and I needed them to be perfect. I focused on my socks whenever I was abused to keep my mind from living through the attacks.

I ran to the cafeteria, desperate to get socks without holes in them, so I asked my friends at the lunch table if anyone would lend me their socks. I tried to explain why socks were so important and that my socks had holes in them. I sobbingly blurted out that I would have to get naked on an exam table for a gynecologist to look at me, but I was allowed to keep my socks on. I literally begged for one of my friends to give me a decent pair of socks. Finally, a friend, Patty, offered me help, saying, "Here Ter, take my socks." I grabbed them and quickly took my holey socks off and offered them to her. She didn't want my socks and said she had Gym class after lunch and would just keep her white gym socks on after that. The others sitting around the lunch table watched silently. I'm sure they were all thinking that it was just another weird day for Terry Harris.

I tried not to talk to my lunch table friends about the sexual things Maskell did to me for fear of his finding out and killing me. I had no idea if he was also making other girls take their clothes off. Or was I the only one? He told me he loved me many times. He said I was special and that he cared deeply about me. Did he tell other girls he loved them too?

After Maskell started to call Linda into his office both with and without me, I knew he was doing things to her, too. I soon figured out that there must be other girls going through the insanity as well. I wondered if he told them, he would kill them if they talked. I began to feel paranoid and thought that maybe Maskell had girls spying on us for him. I had heard that there was a group of girls who reported "unusual" activity to Maskell.

My suspicion was confirmed the next time Maskell ushered me into his office. He wanted to know if I was going to kill myself. I asked him why he would think that. He replied that several girls had reported to him that I gave away a fur coat down in the cafeteria. He added that when people decide to kill themselves, they often give away their belongings, obviously because they won't need them if they were dead. He wanted to know why I didn't want my fur coat anymore. I told him that I had several of my mom's old furs that she didn't wear anymore. I liked to wear her 1950's style beaver fur coat that had large bell-shaped, billowy sleeves. I said I had traded a 1950's mink fur coat to a friend for a pair of leather boots.

My answer seemed to satisfy him. He told me to take my clothes off because it was time for my douche. I was convinced I was going insane.

SUNSHINE CAME SOFTLY...... by Donovan

The next Friday was weird in many ways. My parents told me that morning that I could see my best friend, Linda, over the weekend. My mom said she had spoken to Linda's mom and that the movie *Planet of the Apes* was playing at the Hollywood Theater in Arbutus, near Linda's house. She continued to say that we could see the movie Saturday if we wanted. Mom said I could go home from school with Linda Friday and her mom would drive us to the movie the next day. My brother Mark would pick us up after the movie and bring us back to my house where Linda could spend the night.

I couldn't believe that I was going to be allowed to go out! It had been several months since I had been grounded.

I jumped at the chance. My mom added that Father Maskell had talked to my dad, and told him he thought it would be ok for me to hang out with Linda. Maskell said Linda was a good kid and under his care, just like I was.

I met Linda outside the cafeteria at Keough and talked about those weekend plans. She too was excited to be getting out. After school, we listened to music, *The Rolling Stones – Their Satanic Majesties Request* album, in her room while we discussed what movie to see, not sure that we really wanted to see *Planet of the Apes.*

I was still depressed because I hadn't been allowed out since the "searching of my purse" incident. My long-time boyfriend, Josiah, and I had drifted apart because I was never allowed to see him. My parents didn't like him and they blamed him for the stuff they found in my purse, even though he had nothing to do with that. It didn't help that he wasn't Catholic and had long hair. I loved him! The breakup hit me hard. I was extremely depressed and it showed.

Linda always tried to cheer me up. She told me about a cool guy she knew who actually looked like my old boyfriend. I guess that was supposed to make me feel better. That Saturday, Linda's mom drove us to the Hollywood as we had decided to see *Planet of the Apes*. We had been given permission to eat next door at Mike's Restaurant after the movie. Linda's friends Jim and Ron joined us for the movie and dinner. She introduced me to them as her best friend. After the movie we walked over to the restaurant, sat in booth, and all ordered Mike's famous extra juicy hamburgers and crinkle fries. Jim had very long brown hair and kind hazel eyes. Privately, Linda insisted he looked like my ex, but I didn't think so.

Nevertheless, I did think Jim was cute. He made me laugh as we talked about the movie. Linda went to refill her drink with Ron, who wore dark wire rim glasses, even inside the hamburger place. Over lunch, Ron told us that he had something called Sunshine Acid (LSD) on him and it was amazing. I had sworn off acid and everything else after what happened at the coffee house months ago. However, Ron wouldn't shut up about the Sunshine "wonder" as if it was the best thing in the entire universe. He said the tiniest bit would be amazing and unlike that stuff at the coffee house. He swore we would have a good time.

Linda and I had endured a lot from Maskell. We often talked to each other about what he did and tried to help each other cope. We both wanted an escape from the madness, even if just for a short while. We didn't know if or when we would be allowed out again. In an attempt to justify our actions, we both agreed that we deserved to have some fun. Maybe Sunshine was just what we needed.

Ron also had a bottle of Boone's Farm strawberry wine in his car. After we ate, we walked over to his car and I stuffed the bottle of wine into the billowy coat sleeve of my old fur coat. Linda put a piece of the Sunshine tab in her mouth and gave me the other half. Just then my brother, Mark, pulled up in his gold Chevy Impala. Waving goodbye to Linda's buddies, we jumped in. Mark said he felt like my parole officer and that I had better not mess up on his watch.

Returning home, we walked in the back door leading to the kitchen. Mom was sitting at the red, Formica table waiting to greet us. We talked about the movie and how

Charleston Heston fought off all the apes. Mom had been baking and gave us each a piece of her delicious pumpkin pie. We took pie and glasses of milk up to my room so we could listen to some music while we ate.

At first, we couldn't tell if the Sunshine acid was working. Things seemed pretty normal, except that Linda and I couldn't stop giggling. Everything was funny to us. My purple shag rug, the lamp, the bed and especially my doll collection. Linda got weirded out by my dolls, so I gathered most of them and put them in my large cedarwood closet. I could smell the distinctive cedar wood more than usual because all of my senses were enhanced by the LSD. We laughed hysterically at that. I told her I thought the Sunshine acid was distorting things. She asked me to put the Rolling Stones' album, *Their Satanic Majesties Request* on my stereo because one of the songs, *Like a Rainbow*, was her favorite. We plopped down on my bed to relax and listen to the music.

I had a pretty cool room, decorated with Day-Glo posters and a blacklight. The posters had luminous fluorescent colors, creating a color-saturated vibrance. These types of posters were typically used to advertise rock-concerts. When you turn on an ultraviolet blacklight, the images on these posters literally pop out.

One particular poster depicted the Tower of Babble and lit up like a Christmas tree when the black light was on. This poster portrayed lots of little people lifting bricks and building a tower to God. Linda and I couldn't take our eyes off this poster. We stared at the tower. Linda giggled and said she could hear the little people working on the tower.

I looked down at my purple shag carpet. It was swallowing my feet. A flash of rainbow colors raced across my floor. I sat on the soft carpet with my back against my lavender wall. I noticed the dust gathered on top of my baseboard. I touched the baseboard and it seemed to pull away from the wall. I asked Linda to check it out and she answered, "Ter, that's the most beautiful dust I have ever seen."

I couldn't take my eyes off the cloud-like dust. The music playing combined with the acid. I thought I could hear little people talking and playing in "The land of the dust." I asked Linda to look, but she was still infatuated with the people building the tower. I felt pretty good, but I wasn't sure I really liked what was happening.

Linda could see I was uneasy; she told me that she had heard that drinking orange juice stops the effects of acid. She thought it would either make us come down or crash. Off I headed to the kitchen for orange juice. As I opened my bedroom door, air seemed to rush past me from the hall making a whish sound that made me laugh. The hallway appeared extra-long and very narrow. The more I walked, the longer it seemed to stretch. I finally reached the top of the stairs and groped my way down to the landing. I then managed to navigate the lower steps into the living room.

At this point, I realized that actually getting to the kitchen was a journey fit only for a seasoned tour guide. My brother Mark was watching TV which made the living room glow. I didn't think I could talk, so I raced past the TV and slid into the kitchen. After getting a couple glasses from the cupboard, I turned to the refrigerator. As I reached to open it, the handle melted in my hand. Logic told me this was impossible but there it was, a melty mess. Somehow, I made my way back to my room with the orange juice. That orange juice was refreshing and seemed to lessen the effects of the Sunshine. It had been an interesting night to say the least.

Linda's dad picked her up the following day after we went, still slightly high, to Mass.

YOU NEED YOUR HEAD EXAMINED.... THE SHRINK

The following Monday morning, I met Linda in the cafeteria at school. She seemed fine but I still felt very disoriented. The residual effects of the acid really freaked me out. I headed to my homeroom and flopped into my chair. Within minutes, the voice from the intercom instructed me to report to Father Maskell's office. My heart sank. In my head, I silently begged God to make this stop. I was a robot. I was a total mess.

Maskell was incredibly smart. He saw that something was wrong with me as soon as I walked through his door. I told him I spent the weekend tripping. I never figured out why in the hell I told him, but I did. Worse yet, I shared how

I had heard voices and seen things that weren't really there. I knew it was a mistake as I spoke those words. I just felt so tired of what my life at Keough had become.

Maskell used what I said to convince my dad that he had to take me to a psychiatrist. He told my dad he would arrange for me to start psychiatric treatment with his good friend Dr. Guzman, supposedly a top notch shrink in the area.

The following Saturday Dad drove me to Dr. Guzman's office, located on Wilkens Avenue near St. Agnes Hospital in Baltimore. I had never seen a shrink before and I was anxious. My dad told me not to tell anybody I was seeing a shrink, because they would think I was nuts. He added that it should be a secret; no one needs to know my personal business. I thought to myself that only nuts saw shrinks.

When we entered Guzman's office, Lisa, a friend of mine from Keough, was putting on her coat getting ready to leave. She saw me and blurted out, "Hi, Terry! Did Maskell send you here too?" So much for not telling anybody I was seeing a shrink. My dad was mortified. I just nodded my head and smiled at Lisa as she walked pass us.

Guzman called me into his office. I sat in an upholstered chair facing him. He asked me a series of questions including whether or not my mom dropped me on my head when I was a baby. How in the world would I know that? I was tired of being taken to doctors not knowing what would happen. If I told my dad what was really going on with Maskell, Guzman would be the doctor who would sign me in to Montrose. I tried to act normal, whatever that was, but this whole ordeal was bullshit.

After grilling me about every conceivable moment in my life, Dr. Guzman asked my dad to come into his office. He told my dad that he felt I was a very sick young lady and that I appeared to have the classic symptoms of schizophrenia, hearing voices and seeing things. He told my dad that he would prescribe Thorazine to stop the voices in my head. And all this was *after* I told Guzman I stopped hallucinating once the LSD wore off.

On the way home, we stopped at the pharmacy to fill the prescription so I could start my medication. The Thorazine made me confused and I found it very hard to concentrate on anything. When I read things, I couldn't comprehend what I was reading. It was as if someone else controlled my every thought. I felt like a thing, a toy, a guinea pig.

I had to see Guzman every Saturday morning throughout my junior and part of my senior year. He never abused me sexually but I never got anything helpful out of these sessions. Guzman just asked me questions and encouraged me to talk. I was paranoid so I kept the conversations superficial. I didn't tell him about Maskell sexually abusing me because I was afraid. Maskell was his good friend.

There came a time when Maskell asked my dad if he and Dr. Guzman could administer pure LSD to me and film my reactions. My dad said, "Absolutely Not." I was glad about that.

HYPNOTIZED

I spent a lot of time in Maskell's office. It was typical for me to be in there for four or more hours. I cannot remember many of those hours. It is lost time. I know I was there but couldn't say what happened on many of those long

116

afternoons. I remember his taking off all my clothes (except my socks) and doing sexual things to me or demanding oral sex on most of the days I was there. I remember some things, then I experience lost time and only remember his dropping me off at my house. I haven't been able to remember how I got dressed on most occasions. Sometimes, I think it is merciful that I don't remember everything because what I do remember, is haunting enough.

On one occasion when Maskell had Linda and me in his office together, he asked us if we wanted to be hypnotized. I didn't know much about hypnotism other than what I had seen on TV where people were told to do silly things when they were supposedly under hypnosis. The person who hypnotized them would tell the subject to do things like act like a dog and they would bark and do dog stuff. I wasn't sure if this type of thing was real but I was certain that I couldn't be hypnotized or convinced to do something like that. Both Linda and I said we'd rather not be hypnotized, but "no" was not an option.

Maskell got a watch out of his top desk drawer and told Linda to relax. I watched intently as he talked softly to her and she seemed to fall asleep. He then did the same thing to me. I don't remember much about the rest of that day and neither did Linda other than we went to his office before lunch and left with Maskell late in the day.

He took us to the rectory by way of the now familiar sub shop. Once there, we went up to his room where we ate our subs and listened to his favorite Irish music playing on his small stereo. After we ate, he told Linda to wait on the couch while he took me into his bathroom.

He prepared a douche bag that he kept under his bathroom sink for me and told me to get undressed. He had me lie on my side on the bathroom floor and pushed the plastic tip of the hose attached to the douche bag into my rectum. When he finished administering the enema, he sat me on the toilet and watched me defecate. This was beyond embarrassing to me. Then, to my horror, Maskell insisted on teaching me how to wipe myself. He said many girls wiped their behind from back to front which is wrong because bacteria gets into your vagina and urethra when you wipe that way. Next, he wiped my butt from front to back which is how I always did it anyway. Every time Maskell gave me an enema or a douche I felt dizzy afterward. He always had me clean the toilet before I could leave and then I had to spray his testicles with the can of FDS.

Linda was spared that night, or so I thought. He drove Linda home first, then me. After I got home and up to my bedroom, I called Linda to see how she was doing. Linda told me she felt compelled to give herself an enema as soon as she got home. When I asked her why, she told me she didn't know. I believe Maskell put the enema idea into her mind when he had hypnotized her earlier that day. Why else would she give herself an enema for no apparent reason? Thinking about it, I don't ever remember even having an enema before I met Maskell. Enemas and douches fell into the taboo category of things we never spoke of in our family.

DO YOU REALLY WANT TO HURT ME....Boy George and the Culture Club

During another session in Maskell's office he was sitting at his desk listening to soft music as I walked in. He always had WLIF-FM playing, the kind of music you hear in an elevator. He pulled his chair around to the front of his desk and pulled me into his lap. After he took my clothes off, he pulled my head onto his chest and stroked my hair. He caressed my face and wiped it with a white handkerchief. He said he liked how the handkerchief stayed white because I didn't wear makeup. He said he wanted to keep me pure. I told him my stomach hurt, hoping he would leave me alone that day. But he pushed me up and went to the rear corner of his office to get something. The lights were dim, but I could see he was pouring me a drink as my shaky hands lit my Kool cigarette.

He told me to sit on the floor in front of his desk so he could examine me. As he touched me all over, I felt sick to my stomach. I wanted to vomit. I couldn't think. He said I was special to him and he hugged me.

He started to touch my abdomen all over pressing down on my bare skin. I wondered what he was going to do next. He told me he was checking to see if I had appendicitis as he pushed down on my right side. I told him my stomach felt better and nothing hurt. The situation was surreal. Maskell worked his hands up my abdomen and said he could feel something. Suddenly, he blurted out, "You are full of crap! That's what's wrong with you, you are full of crap." He got up and ran around to the back of his desk and got something out of one of the drawers. I sat up scared out of my mind and backed up against the wall. He lunged toward me saying he had something to help clean me out. I couldn't see what was in his hand; I ran away from him to the other side of his desk. He laughed and tackled me to the floor and inserted something into my vagina. He opened the door leading to the bathroom inside his office and sat me down hard on the toilet seat. He pulled his chair around to watch me, but I just sat there. He got angry as time passed and I didn't have a bowel movement. I told him I didn't have to go. He said he inserted a suppository in me and I should go. It was in my vagina and he had intended to insert it in my anus. I didn't tell him where it really was because I was so afraid.

The next thing I remember, I was looking at the clock and seeing that it was almost 4 pm, and school was long over for the day. Confused, I realized that I had been in Maskell's office for another entire day. Whatever happened after the toilet incident is beyond me, but I always remembered everything about the suppository and his watching me in the bathroom. As time passed, I learned that Maskell had other games he was going to play with me in his bathroom.

HALLOWEEN 1970

Linda came over to spend Halloween night with me. After dinner we had planned to hang out in my room and listen to music. Maskell had other ideas. Earlier that day, he had called my dad to ask him if he could take me on a Halloween police run. Maskell told my dad that he was the police chaplain and there was usually a lot of action on Halloween. It was a chance for him to show me how the police dealt with delinquents and troublemakers. It would be kind of a "scared straight" lesson in case I ever decided to act out again. Maskell had already gotten permission to take Linda along too so I'd have company.

Maskell arranged to pick both of us up at my house. Linda and I got dressed in my room to go out with him as if we were going on a date. He even came to my front door to get us like a date would.

We did see action that night. Maskell took us to a wooded area in nearby Patapsco Park where several police cars were parked. The police had broken up a "teen parking ring." I waited in Maskell's car with Linda while Maskell and the police ordered the teens out of their cars. They made the couples line up and frisked them. Maskell said demeaning things to the teens like how pathetic they were, lusting after each other. One girl's pants looked wet and Maskell let out a belly laugh saying, "Look this one pissed herself." Finally, a cop told the teens they could leave and I watched them disappear down the road.

Maskell came back to his car, opened the back door and pulled Linda out. He told me to stay in the back seat. Suddenly, my door opened and a man dressed as a cop got in and pulled my jeans and underpants off. He pushed me down onto the seat as he ripped open my blouse. He started to kiss my neck. I could feel his hot breath on my face as he pushed himself inside me. He hurt me. I started to cry and begged him to stop. His heavy belt and what I think was his holster, were rubbing against my thigh, hard. After what seemed like an eternity, he switched places with a second cop. This cop rolled me over and told me to stay still. He pushed his penis into my anus and I screamed with pain. I felt like I was watching my body from above. I saw Maskell standing outside the car and hoped he would stop this. I could hear his deep voice laughing. I focused on his voice. Why wouldn't he help me? Finally, the second cop finished and left.

I struggled to get dressed just as the car door flew open on the side where Linda had been sitting. She slid across the seat and we huddled very close. She was sobbing. We held hands tightly, both crying in excruciating pain, not knowing what to expect next.

Maskell got back into the car and told us to shut up with the crying. He drove us home to my house. He went to the front door with us and told my dad there hadn't been much going on that Halloween, but we did get to see some hot spots where some kids were caught necking. Linda and I slipped past my parents. I managed to smile reassuringly at my mom as we went upstairs to my room. Linda and I held hands and sat up all night, quietly staring into space. I never knew what they did to Linda that night; she could never talk about it.

DANCING IN THE DARK.......by Bruce Springfield

I was getting called out of class about three times a week, anytime Maskell wanted to see me. To 'counsel' me. Sometimes I was called out to report to the nurse's office where Maskell would be waiting with his awful grin. On those days, Maskell would walk me down the hall to his office at the other end of the school. We would walk past the principal's office where I could clearly see the school secretaries through the window there. We would pass the library where other students were gathered. Couldn't they see me? Didn't they know? I wondered how many people knew and did nothing.

Once in his office, Maskell repeated that if I told anyone anything, no one would ever believe me over him. He said I was nothing but a delinquent druggie and he was a respected priest. He showed me his gun and told me he would use it to kill me and nobody would ever see me again. I'd simply be listed as another runaway brat.

He told me to get in his big blue car and drove me to the rectory. He always bought me my meatball sub and a Coke which I usually ate while sitting on his couch. Maskell held me close in his lap and told me he loved me and cared about me. For a time, I wondered if Maskell could truly love me in some twisted way. Was this a relationship? I now believe that by proclaiming his love for me, Maskell was grooming me to somehow make me believe I belonged with him.

That evening he put his Irish music on the stereo and danced about his rectory room smiling and laughing. He pulled me up from the couch so I could dance with him while he held me tight and whispered how I was truly special to him. He loved to sing along with his music about Sweet Molly Malone selling cockles and mussels in Dublin's fair city.... To this day I cannot listen to that song without remembering those bizarre times with Maskell at the rectory.

Suddenly, he said we had to get me cleaned up as he led me into his now familiar bathroom where the cold tiles greeted me. Maskell began to put water and the Massengill powder into the douche bag. My blood ran cold. My mind was trying to make sense of why he was giving me another douche. Could he care for me in his own depraved way? It was so weird to endure the douches. I often thought if he cared for me, maybe he wouldn't kill me. Maybe he would let me live.

The daily Thorazine pill seemed to make things increasingly worse. I had difficulty trying to focus. I felt like I was really losing my mind. I had no say in anything that was happening to me and I just wanted it to end. I now know that believing that Maskell cared for me in some eccentric way was a form of self-protection. I believe my mind was attempting to rationalize what he did to me. It was my way to survive the insanity.

THE CHAPEL

Maskell had a door in the rear of his office that led directly into the chapel at Keough. He sometimes took me in there and locked the chapel doors that led to the school hallway. The first time he did this, he lifted me up onto the altar, ejaculated into his chalice that was meant to hold the body and blood of Christ during Mass and forced me to drink it to "let the Holy Spirit into your heart, Terry."

When I left the chapel, I saw a girl who was a year ahead of me at Keough go into Maskell's office. Later that day I saw the same girl walking swiftly toward the library. I managed to catch up to her. I told her I was Terry and I was often told to report to Father Maskell's office. She told me her name was Amy and confided in me that she too had to see Maskell for counseling. Not often, but numerous times.

Amy told me that when Maskell called her into his office he took her into the chapel and used the altar as a gynecological exam table. I understood exactly what she was saying to me. Amy went on to say that Maskell gave her pelvic exams on the altar, that she was so used to his doing it that she thought of him as her doctor. I shared things with her about what happened to me in the chapel. Apparently, Maskell had told both of us that he had studied to be a doctor but was called by God to do greater work as a priest. I wondered where God was now. Could he see what was happening at Keough?

I saw Amy from time to time in the cafeteria. We got to be good friends and would sneak out of lunch and go to the auditorium where she showed me how to climb onto the cat walks above the stage, where she smoked pot. I joined her on several occasions instead of eating lunch in the cafeteria. During those times, we shared Maskell stories and even laughed about some of the things he said to us. The gallows humor was another coping mechanism I used to deal with my abuse. One afternoon Amy told me she was pregnant. She left Keough abruptly before graduation and I envied her for getting out.

EVENING PHONE CALLS

Maskell had total control of me both in and out of school. He would often call me at my home in the evening to further "counsel" me. Of course, my dad believed he was acting in my best interest to help me because that is what Maskell promised him he would do. During one such evening I was experiencing hallucinations and hearing things much like I had when on LSD.

That afternoon I had spent the entire day in Maskell's office. Although I knew that to be true, I couldn't remember what had occurred while I had been there. I now believe that I had been drugged that day. It was about 7p.m. when Maskell called me. His voice on the other end of the line was calming to the extent he made me feel more normal, like I wasn't losing my mind completely. I told him about strange things I was seeing in my bedroom. Geometric shapes seemed to be floating by as I spoke. Maskell listened intently as I explained the triangles, circles and squares around me. He asked me many questions before instructing me to sleep. That was one of the weirdest evenings I experienced back then. Looking back, I wonder if I had been part of a mind control experiment of some kind.

THE ANATOMY LESSON

Maskell often gave me psychological tests. Sometimes he would call my friend, Linda, to come in with me during these tests. He had us look at ink blots and tell him what we saw in them. I always said I saw my beloved beagle, Yappy.

Linda usually said she saw a storm cloud which was strangely appropriate, I thought.

One day as we were looking at the ink blots, Maskell asked us if we ever looked at ourselves "down there." We remained silent. He gave us sodas in a paper cup and let us smoke a cigarette to unwind. I knew what "down there" meant and was beginning to feel nauseous.

When I finished my smoke, he told me to take my clothes off and lie on the floor. I kept my socks on which strangely provided a small sense of comfort. I remember being grateful that his floor was carpeted. He told Linda to sit next to me and she could keep her clothes on. He pushed my legs apart and told Linda to take a closer look. She said she didn't feel right doing this. Maskell insisted, saying we should know everything we could about our bodies and he wanted her to know what our private parts looked like. He used his fingers to touch my labia and named my parts one by one. This is Terry's labia, this is her clitoris, this is… He held a mirror up to my body parts and insisted I watch.

I started to feel dizzy. I know now that Maskell put something in that Coke he gave me because I always got dizzy after I drank one. He started to touch my abdomen. He guided Linda's hand over my belly and pushed it down on me. He asked her if she could feel it. She said, "Feel what?" to which he replied, "Crap, Terry's full of crap." Again??? I thought. He pulled me upright and made me eat something that tasted like chocolate, which I later learned was a laxative, Ex-Lax. I don't remember getting dressed but somehow, Linda and I made our way to the cafeteria. We ate in shamed silence.

SAVING LINDA

About a month before graduation, Linda came to school drunk. I learned that she had a fight with her boyfriend and got her older brother, Dennis, to buy her some red port wine. I thought she must have drunk the entire bottle because she could barely walk. A few of our friends from the lunch table took her into the woods between Keough and Cardinal Gibbons in an attempt to hide her until school ended for the day. One of Maskell's spies must have told him that Linda was drunk because we heard that he was looking for her. A girl managed to arrange for a friend to pick Linda up from the woods and take her to her house in nearby Morrell Park.

A short while later, I saw Maskell in the hall next to the general office. He stopped me and demanded I tell him where Linda was. I knew that Linda had been upset about things and was counting the days leading up to our graduation.

I told Maskell I didn't know where she was and even if I did, I wasn't going to tell him. I told him I was getting out of there in a few days and I wasn't going to put up with his shit anymore and he could shoot me if he wanted to. Maskell slapped me right in front of the office where the school secretary had to see me. He said, "I'm going to fry your ass, Harris. If you know where Linda is you better tell me." I was defiant, "So, you can do things to her too?" He stormed off. I was shaking all over. I later learned that one of his spies told him where Linda was, and he drove to Morrell Park and picked her up. Apparently, he knocked on the door where Linda was hiding, and the girl who lived there felt intimidated and afraid, so she let Maskell in. Linda told me later that he took her back to his office at Keough where he raped her nine ways from Sunday. He threw her around like a ragdoll while raping her anally and she was still bleeding.

I hadn't been called to report to Maskell for several weeks but I was afraid he would kill me for standing up to him when Linda was drunk. I too counted the days leading to my getting out of the hellhole known as Keough.

CHAPTER 7

TEENAGE MOTHERHOOD

I accepted my situation, that I was a pregnant teenager planning to run away and marry another teenager, Jim Gagne, whom I had known only a few months. I couldn't see any other way to deal with my circumstances. I had met Jim in the Morrell Park neighborhood three months earlier, while Linda and I were visiting a friend there after school. Linda knew Jim from the neighborhood and introduced us. Jim and I seemed to be on the same wavelength. Neither of us had clear ideas of what we wanted out of life. I told him about Maskell and what it was like to be stuck at Keough with no clue as to what would happen next. Jim wanted to confront Maskell, but I managed to talk him out of that. I told him I believed Maskell had a nun killed, and it was best to just stay away from him.

Jim and I enjoyed doing things together like visiting the Baltimore City Zoo and Walters Art Gallery downtown. We liked the same music and often went to concerts at what was then called the Baltimore Civic Center. The Civic Center was renovated and renamed the Baltimore Arena in the 1980's. It was only a short distance from the then newly established Inner Harbor. In 2003 the Baltimore Arena became the 1st Mariner Arena and remained so until 2013. Royal Farms bought the naming rights in 2014 and the arena remains a popular venue, seating up to 14,000 people under their name. Back in the 1970's Jim and I saw the rock groups Kiss, Led Zeppelin and Alice Cooper there.

One thing led to another and here I was expecting a child, not even knowing where I was going in life or who I really was. I focused on the reality that I had only a week left at Keough before I would be free. Free from Maskell and all the craziness that had become my life. I had not thought about college for a long time. I did not gain a shred of education at Keough those last two years. Nothing to prepare me for college. Instead, I adopted a survival mentality to deal with my plight on a day-by-day basis.

On May 22, 1972, I married Jim Gagne at the Sexton United Methodist Church in Morrell Park. I wore bell-bottom blue jeans which I had decorated with silver studs forming a vine up the sides. I added embroidered ruby colored roses around the vines. Jim plucked a bright yellow buttercup from just outside the church and lovingly placed it behind my right ear. We stood before an elderly preacher with Jim's mom, Mildred, standing behind us, and nervously exchanged our wedding vows, me in a barely audible whisper. This was not the wedding I had dreamed of as a little girl, but it was my new normal and I had to deal with it.

Jim and I left the church and took a transit bus into the city. Hand in hand, we walked along the busy Baltimore streets, full of bumper-to-bumper rush hour traffic. I was tired and scared, not knowing what to expect. Jim had told me about a really cool place where we could live. It was an old stone house with many rooms that was built in the late 1800's at 1010 North Calvert Street. He said the house was divided into apartments and his friend, Bob, lived there along with about ten other people. Bob told Jim that everyone in the house shared chores, like preparing meals and keeping the place clean. Rent wouldn't be a problem because we would only have to pay about $90 a month for our space.

I was hesitant as I approached the tall, jet-black, varnished door leading into the nineteenth century house. On the right, there was a shining brass door knob that glistened like gold as the evening sun bounced off it. Jim reached for the door knob just as his friend Bob was coming out. I had met Bob back in Morrell Park several months earlier and found him to be upbeat and pleasant. He told us he was headed out to the corner store to pick up some spaghetti noodles and garlic bread for our dinner and that the others were expecting us. Once inside, Jim introduced me to several of his other friends who lived there. Everyone was very friendly as they welcomed us into their 'city commune'. Jan, a girl not much older than I, took us to our efficiency apartment on the third floor. I quickly learned that an efficiency apartment consisted of one large room containing a kitchen, living, and sleeping area with a modest separate bathroom. Jan smiled as she said we had one of the best 'studio' apartments there and it had a brick fire place. I wondered how I would sleep as my eyes were drawn to two tall windows overlooking the busy street just outside our building. The only thing between the house and the thunderous traffic was the steep concrete steps leading into the house. There was no front yard with flowering shrubs and towering shade trees like the one I grew up with.

I gazed out at the passing cars and noticed a pay phone just a few houses away, near the corner store. My heart sank as I realized I needed to call my mom to tell her why I wouldn't be coming home that night. My mom loved me unconditionally and was always there for me. I felt an overwhelming sadness and cried as I walked to the phone. My mind was racing through all the wonderful childhood memories I had growing up. Here I was, I thought, 18, on my own, and soon to be a mom myself. I dropped my dime into the phone's pay slot and slowly dialed the numbers with my shaky finger.

My mom's voice on the other end of the line grew quiet as I told her I was married and that I was staying with a group of friends in an apartment on North Calvert Street in downtown Baltimore. It was like dropping a bomb on her. She was devastated. She begged me to promise to finish school so I could get my diploma. I sobbed as I told her I would continue to attend Keough for the last few days of school and graduate as scheduled on Sunday, June 4, 1972. I also agreed to meet with her and my dad at Jim's mom's house in Morrell Park to talk about everything on Saturday, just a few days away. I had not yet told her I was pregnant. I was terrified.

My mom and dad arrived early that gloomy Saturday and my mother-in-law, Mildred, invited them in. My mom was visibly shaken. My dad asked Mildred why she helped us do such a thing as getting married, without letting them know. Knowing that my dad was a lawyer, Jim's mom nervously blurted out that she was only trying to help and that I was pregnant. There were a lot of tears that day. It was one of the worse days of my life.

My dad was a realist and sought to make our situation the best it could be. Mom worried about my safety and hated that I was living with a bunch of hippies in downtown Baltimore. My dad found a small apartment for us in a nice neighborhood on Francis Ave in Halethorpe, just five miles from my childhood home on Nottingham Road. Ironically, the apartment was just a few blocks away from my best friend, Linda. Jim and I were able to move in there with a few household necessities and started our married life as normally as possible.

Luckily, Jim found a job within walking distance to our apartment as a forklift driver for the Maryland Housing Lumber Company. He was just eighteen years old and had minimal job training. We were happy in our little home. I soon gave birth to a baby boy we named Jeremy and I quickly adapted to my new life as a young mother. I was nervous about all the things I had to do to make sure my baby was well cared for. My Mom asked my dad to pick up Jeremy and me several mornings a week before he left for his law office and drive us to her house so she could help me with the baby. She knew I wasn't getting much sleep because I had told her the baby was colicky and cried all night. I was able to grab a short nap while Mom bathed and fed him. These days turned out to be magical for Mom and me. We became remarkably close. She became my best friend and I treasured my time with her and my son.

I never spoke of Keough or Maskell or anything that had happened during my high school years. Instead, I lived each day as it came. You could say I practiced mindfulness.

Dad referred to Jim and me as kids with kids and shook his head a lot. It was not easy, but it was real. Jim and I remained married until his death sixteen years and four kids later.

IN THE BEGINNING

Jim worked several menial jobs early on in our marriage. He continued to drive a forklift at the lumber company until I became pregnant again just six months after the birth of my son. Someone told me at the time that I was having Irish twins. Naive, I didn't know what that meant so I looked it up and learned it was a slang expression used to describe siblings who are born less than a year apart to the same mother. Irish

Catholics were not supposed to practice birth control and when many of them immigrated to the US in the nineteenth century it was common for them to have children born less than twelve months apart. Thus, the term Irish twins, came about and my close pregnancies fit the bill.

Our modest Halethorpe apartment was pretty small and only had one bedroom. A second baby would make the place really cramped. Realizing how limited our space was, Jim's mom suggested we stay with her in her Morrell Park townhouse, which had three bedrooms. She said my babies could each have their own room and Jim and I could sleep in her newly renovated basement. The basement had a spacious bedroom combined with a sitting room adjacent to a separate laundry room complete with a washer and dryer. Mildred added, reassuringly, that this set up would be only for a little while, until we were back on our feet. Once again, my reality was not the life I dreamed of as a young girl, but it was my life and I accepted my situation.

It wasn't long before Jim found a job in a small machine shop located in South Baltimore. He had taken a machine shop program in high school where he learned to operate precision metal-cutting equipment to produce metal parts from mechanical blueprints. He had experience using cutting and measuring tools such as lathes, drill presses, vices, micrometers and milling machines. His new employer was quite impressed with Jim's training and started him out with good pay and health benefits. We were so very excited about his new job!

In the Spring of 1974, we welcomed our second child, a beautiful girl whom we named Lisa Marie. Both of our children were happy and healthy and adored by their grandparents. I felt almost normal and I was happy. Things were finally looking up. But not for long. While using a drill press without a safety shield, Jim injured his hand. His hand required stitches and he was laid off because he was unable to perform his job duties.

Even though there was a 1970 law designed to assure safe working conditions for employees under the Occupational Safety and Health Administration (OSHA), many smaller businesses had not yet fully complied with the regulations which required installing safety shields on dangerous machinery. Things were tough because Jim could not work until his hand healed, and even then, we weren't sure he could continue at the machine shop. Buying groceries and paying the pediatrician bills became increasingly difficult. We wanted to prove we could take care of our own needs, but things were looking grim.

I applied for government assistance and found we qualified for food stamps, Medicaid, and temporary cash assistance. I didn't know much about government programs for poor people, but I soon learned that a lot of people looked down on me because I was "on the dole." This arduous experience turned out to be a good thing down the road, because it inspired me to become a Social Worker, so I could help other poor people maintain a degree of dignity.

On one occasion my neighbor, Natalie, invited me to go grocery shopping with her and the kids. We had become close as stay-at-home moms caring for our young children. I didn't have a car and enjoyed Natalie's company, so I jumped at the chance to spend the afternoon grocery shopping together.

I had food stamps but was embarrassed to use them because it took so long to tear them from their books at the checkout. Back then people didn't shop with bank debit cards and the electronic food stamp benefits transfer card did not exist. I had no other choice but to shop with my food stamps because I didn't have any cash. I thought if I tore the stamps out ahead of time, I could save time and not hold up the often-judgmental shoppers behind me at the grocery store.

My plan backfired when I reached the checkout line. The cashier refused to accept my food stamps because she did not witness their being torn from the books. Unknown to me, my government-issued food stamp identification card had numbers that corresponded with numbers imprinted on the front of each food stamp book. Apparently, I was supposed to tear each stamp from its book while the cashier witnessed me doing so. I learned that this rule was in force because some food stamp recipients sold loose food stamps at a reduced rate, such as 50 cents on a dollar, to desperate poor people. Thus, it was technically illegal for a store to knowingly accept loose food stamps. I thought to myself that

I must look like a hardened criminal standing there with my toddler and my new baby trying to buy fresh vegetables and formula. I did not even know how to be poor. Live and learn, right?

The checkout line started to back up, which I dreaded. I could hear the women waiting in line behind me mumbling nasty comments about me under their breath. The store manager came over to confirm what the cashier had said and reiterate that my loose food stamps were voided. He added, "How am I supposed to know you didn't buy these on the black market?" I started crying.

Natalie had finished paying for her groceries and when she saw me crying with my kids, she came over and paid for my groceries with her own money. I vowed to change my living standards at that moment. I decided that somehow, I would go back to school so I could get a decent job and support my family.

About six months later, Jim finally managed to get a great job at the Gould Corporation which was awarded government defense contracts. He became the quality control engineer there and was responsible for inspecting finished products and measuring all the parts with micrometers and digital calipers before they went out to the military. The job paid well and included medical insurance which enabled us to pay for our own food and other necessities. We did not have much and lived paycheck to paycheck, but things were finally looking up.

It wasn't long before I found myself pregnant again. My pregnancies were never seen as a happy, wonderful event by my family and friends. I endured hurtful comments like:

"Haven't you heard of birth control."

"What are you going to do about it this time?"

"I know a doctor who will get rid of it for you."

I spent a lot of time crying each time I found myself pregnant, and if it hadn't been for the support of my mom, I don't think I would have survived. My mom was always there for me. She never gave up on me. She showed me loving support each time I got pregnant. She never criticized me for getting myself deeper into poverty by having too many kids. She always told me to hold my head high, and she proudly welcomed each of my children with open arms. The unconditional love she gave me throughout my entire life instilled in me the strength and courage to conquer anything this world threw at me.

My third child, Christy is a beautiful and loving soul and I couldn't imagine my life without her. Lisa was proud to be an older sister and loved helping me take care of her new baby sister. Things were good, but I realized our resources were being stretched. After Christy was born, I underwent a tubal ligation so I could never get pregnant again. I felt like my little family was complete. Jim had a great job and we were happy.

Several weeks after Christy was born, I felt ill and nauseated, especially in the morning. I also felt lightheaded and dizzy. These symptoms were not new to me as I felt this way every time I got pregnant. I confided in Natalie and she took me to the local drug store to get one of those then-new home pregnancy test kits. Imagine my shock when I saw that my test read positive. I revealed my situation to Jim and we made an appointment to see Dr. Kingston, my gynecologist.

He confirmed my suspicions and told me I was about six weeks into my fourth pregnancy despite the fact that just a week prior he had declared my tubal ligation procedure a success. As Jim and I sat in his office, Dr. Kingston offered to perform an abortion without charge. He insisted that I was sterile from the tubal ligation and that this egg just slipped through. I am far from religious, but I said if this baby wants to be born in this god-forsaken world, who am I to deny it?

I had had an abortion during my junior year at Keough. I could never talk about it nor could I ever forgive myself. It crushed my soul, and I cannot speak of it still, not even in this book. I knew I could never do such a thing again and that I would have this baby. Strangely, I felt as though this baby could be the soul I had extinguished.

To be clear, I strongly believe in pro-choice, and that women have the right to decide what is best for them.

I picked myself up and put on a positive face. As my pregnancy began to show, I faced those same hurtful comments from some so-called friends and I became extremely depressed. Once again, my mom put her loving arms around me and told me it was wonderful that I was going to have a new baby to play with Christy. I cried. I cried a lot. But as Mom told me to do, I always held my head high and told my critics, "What's another face in the crowd?"

I named my fourth child after my mom, Annette. I think of her as my miracle baby. She is a wonderful gift and having her was the greatest decision I have ever made.

INTRUSIVE MASKELL MEMORIES

Living life as a young mom made me feel complete, but there were days when haunting memories of Maskell filled my head. What made things worse was that I learned that Maskell was still functioning as a priest at the nearby St. Clement Parish where my neighbor, Natalie, and her children attended Mass. I had already told her that Maskell was a pervert and that he had sexually assaulted me continuously at Keough. I felt the need to reiterate that as well as to warn her that he was a dangerous monster. She should never allow her children to be alone with him or near him, at all. I found it to be therapeutic to talk about what Maskell had done to me and to make sure Maskell could not hurt my friend. It became a constant struggle to keep these intrusive memories from consuming my life.

Eventually I was able to block out most of what Maskell did to me. I embraced my newfound role as a wife and mother and loved my family deeply. Things were good. My days were consumed with caring for my family. I loved every day I spent with my children and took joy in watching them grow.

A LUMP

Jim and I both had spring birthdays. Mine was April 29th and his just nine days later on May 8th. We liked to celebrate together by having family picnics at Patapsco Park where the kids could enjoy the playground and explore the woods with us. Our celebration didn't last long. In 1982, the year we both turned twenty-eight, was the year Jim became gravely ill.

Jim started to experience pain when walking, and we noticed a small lump in his leg just above his knee. The lump was painful for him and it could be moved around when touched. We went to several different doctors, seeking a diagnosis. We were told everything from the lump's being the result of a spider bite to its being harmless fatty tissue. I made an appointment with a highly-recommended internist, Dr. John Edman. He told us that the lump was a detached muscle. He recommended a series of ultrasound treatments to break it up. Jim saw this doctor several times a week for those treatments designed to disperse and disintegrate the lump. Instead, the lump kept getting larger until Jim could no longer go to work.

My brother Mark and I were always very close. He is a doctor and worked as a neonatologist at Johns Hopkins at the time we discovered Jim's lump. One afternoon, I asked Mark to review Jim's medical records I had copied. I wanted his opinion why the lump was getting bigger, instead of smaller with the ultrasound treatments. Mark took me aside that Sunday at our mom's house and told me he believed Jim had cancer and that a biopsy of that lump should have been done months before. He added that in medical school they had a saying that whenever there is a lump, stick it with a needle (to get a sample of tissue to biopsy.)

I asked the internist treating Jim during his next appointment if he could biopsy the lump to determine why it continued to grow. He didn't take me seriously. After all, what could an unsophisticated 28-year-old woman know about medicine and biopsies? He said it wasn't necessary to biopsy the lump, because the ultrasound treatment would resolve the problem. He insisted that we give the treatment more time to work. Giving us some cream to rub on the area, he sent us on our way. This was bullshit, I thought.

I learned that there are doctors called oncologists who specialize in the treatment of lumps. I made an appointment with a highly recommended female oncologist at nearby St Agnes Hospital in Baltimore, Dr. Alice Burger. When I took Jim into her office, she was disturbed at the size of the tumor in his leg. I didn't even have to ask; she immediately arranged for a needle biopsy. We went home and waited anxiously for the results. The oncologist called a few days later and asked us to come into her office. There she told us that Jim had an exceedingly rare form of cancer called myxoid lipo-sarcoma. This diagnosis was profoundly serious.

After further examinations, we learned that the cancerous tumor in Jim's leg had metastasized to his chest; there was a second mass there. The oncologist informed us that the cancer was terminal. Shocked to borderline hysteria, I asked her if anything could be done to get rid of the cancer. She told us she was deeply sorry, but it was her professional opinion that Jim had about three months to live. I was not ready to accept this prognosis.

I called Johns Hopkins Oncology Department as soon as we got home and told whoever would listen that I had four young children and I was told my husband had terminal cancer with only three months to live. I begged that he be seen and evaluated by somebody... anybody. I knew Hopkins was the best hospital in Maryland (probably in the country) and I believed they could help us. Jim sat quietly on the couch with the kids while I continued to reach out for someone to help us. Finally, I got an appointment for a consultation at the Johns Hopkins Oncology Center in Baltimore the next day.

We met a compassionate oncologist, Dr. Dan Stewart, at Hopkins, who explained how he worked with a team of doctors there. These doctors were proactive and willing to develop a plan to treat Jim instead of just giving up. They quickly came up with a protocol after reviewing Jim's medical records. First, an oncological surgeon would remove the main tumor from the leg. Then a thoracic surgeon would operate on the tumor in his chest where the cancer had metastasized. Depending on the outcomes of the operations, Jim would begin chemotherapy followed by radiation treatments.

We elected to move forward with the plan to save Jim. The surgeons were able to successfully extract the tumor from his leg, but in the process had to remove most of the muscles in his upper thigh. He would need a leg brace to walk again, but we felt that was a small price to pay to get rid of the cancer. We were cautiously optimistic.

CHAPTER 8

BEAT THE CLOCK

Complications from the first procedure caused Jim's thoracic surgery to be postponed. The setback in his treatment was due to the incision on his leg not healing properly. Jim developed a fissure at the incision site, a narrow opening deep into the wound along his femur. The fissure would fill up with fluid, literally blowing the bandages off his leg on a daily basis. His doctor and nurses taught me how to pack the fissure with strips of gauze soaked in saline solution. The packing would need to be changed often. My oldest daughter, Lisa, would often help me change the dressing by slowly feeding me the saline-soaked gauze as I packed it into the open wound. I also had to administer morphine to Jim around the clock because his incessant pain was unbearable. This ordeal continued for several months. Meanwhile, the metastasized tumor in his chest continued to grow.

Jim's medical team finally called us to discuss how best to speed up the healing process in his leg. This was imperative in order to proceed with the surgical removal of the mass devouring the tissue in his chest. The doctor recommended that Jim get a computerized tomography (CT) scan (CAT-scan), which takes a series of X-rays from different angles around the area in question. This then-new procedure uses computer processing to create cross-sectional images of bones, soft tissue and blood vessels in the body. The doctor told us these visual 'slices' would give the surgeon a clearer, more detailed picture than just X-rays.

Jim's CAT-scan showed that the tumor in his chest was pressing up against his pericardium, the fibrous membrane enclosing the heart, and would kill him if it got much bigger. One option to alleviate the leg issue was to amputate it. Before resorting to that, one surgeon, Doctor Oscar Miller, suggested wiring the incision shut and putting Jim on massive IV antibiotics. Even if this didn't hold, it would enable the thoracic surgeon, Doctor Bradley Carson, to remove the threatening tumor in Jim's chest.

Doctor Miller admitted Jim and scheduled the leg procedure the next morning. I spent the night with him in the hospital in an attempt to keep him calm. This was difficult because I was consumed with worry...about Jim as well as about my youngest daughter, Annette, who had been admitted that same day to a different hospital for a high fever caused by severe tonsilitis. My mom stayed by Annette's side and provided me with regular reports on her condition, as the evening approached. Fortunately, IV antibiotics administered to Annette caused her fever to break and she was released from the hospital that evening. Thus, I was able to maintain a positive face while sitting with Jim. I elected not to tell him about Annette's ordeal since she was well on her way to a full recovery and he was loopy from the morphine dripping into his IV.

When morning came, I walked alongside Jim as the nurse wheeled him into surgery. I was then directed to the family waiting room where his mom had been sitting. Nine hours later, the lead thoracic surgeon, Dr. Carson, entered the family waiting room to discuss the outcome of the chest surgery with us. He said he was able to successfully "debulk" the tumor, which reduced its mass. He further explained that Jim's tumor looked like a cauliflower and, as expected, it had grown very close to the surrounding organs. This made it impossible to remove the entire tumor without causing catastrophic organ damage. Additionally, the tumor had wrapped around several of Jim's ribs and was beginning to enter the diaphragm, necessitating the removal of two ribs. Dr. Bradley remained optimistic and told us that with chemotherapy and subsequent radiation treatments, any remaining tumor should shrink significantly, and Jim should have years ahead of him.

About an hour later, a nurse told me Jim had been taken to the recovery room, where they were getting him situated so I could see him. She warned me that his appearance could seem alarming because he had to remain in an upright position which can appear extremely uncomfortable to non-medical persons. Additionally, although the ventilator had been removed, Jim needed to use an incentive spirometer device to exercise his lungs. He needed to breathe into the spirometer every twenty minutes to keep the alveoli (small air sacs) in his lungs open. He also had a chest tube leading out from the surgical site to allow excess fluid and air to exit the chest. The nurse explained that the surgeon would remove the chest tube after the drainage had stopped and the surgeon was confident air was not escaping. This could take three to four days.

Jim was in a great deal of pain and told me he would rather die than go through any more surgery. The doctor kept him pretty much sedated for several days. I was thankful for that.

Jim was discharged about three weeks later and provided with detailed instructions on home care. I scheduled his chemotherapy appointments, which would begin in about ten days. I wrote everything in a journal which I started shortly after we were told Jim had three months to live. Almost a year had passed since we first learned about the cancer. I found it cathartic to write about what Jim was going through. I called my journal "One Man's Battle."

Noooooooooooooo

Just when things seemed to be falling into place with Jim's treatments, my mom told me she found a lump in her breast. I assured her that it was probably nothing, even though I expected the worst. I had learned that the worst is easier to digest if you are ready for it. My dad took my mom to an oncologist and we soon learned that she had advanced breast cancer that had infiltrated her lymph nodes. She was just fifty-eight years old. I had become incredibly close to my mom to the point that I felt I couldn't deal with life without her. It is difficult to describe how the news of her cancer affected me.

I felt as though another person was hearing this awful news. I couldn't accept it. I experienced night terrors with anxiety episodes of extreme panic that woke me up. I found myself thinking about being in Maskell's office. These intruding thoughts haunted me, and I experienced remembering more details about what happened during my Keough years.

My mom underwent a modified radical mastectomy. The surgeon removed all her right breast tissue along with the lymph nodes in her armpit. She never complained. Not once. Mom started chemotherapy shortly after her mastectomy. I drove her there because I wanted to be close to her as much as possible. She was self-conscious about her appearance when her hair started to fall out. I had already experienced this dreadful side effect of chemotherapy with Jim. I bought him a nice realistic wig to boost his ego. I wanted to do the same for my mom. One afternoon before she started her cancer treatments, I took her shopping for a honey-blonde wig with both light and dark highlights that would make it look realistic. She was hesitant at first but soon loved the wig. We also bought some comfortable loose clothes for her to wear during her chemotherapy.

I wanted to divert my mom's attention from her upcoming cancer treatments. Mom had told me about three months prior that she wanted to re-decorate her gloomy bedroom that hadn't been painted for many years. The walls were once a cheerful shade of royal blue and had faded into a gloomy grayish hue. So, before we went home, I suggested we check out the store's paint department to see the available colors for her bedroom. We looked through all the color charts and Mom decided to get a delicate shade of baby blue latex paint that was sure to brighten her bedroom. As the clerk mixed our paint, I grabbed some rollers, brushes and a few other items to help me complete the job.

We started to leave the department store with our purchases and came to a huge sale on curtains and drapes. I suggested we look for new curtains for the two bedroom-windows and French doors, that lead from her bedroom out to her balcony. I thought the doors would look great with drapes that matched the curtains. Mom picked out a beautiful set of drapes that had a bohemian floral pattern, with both warm red tones mixed with calming blue hues. Perfect! We bought the drapes and two sets of matching window curtains and headed home for lunch. I said I'd paint the bedroom over the weekend with the help of my oldest daughter, Lisa. We could hang the curtains after that and it would be beautiful.

I found that small things do wonders for both the caregiver and the patient. Re-decorating my mom's bedroom was something I could control, and since I had no power over her cancer, I needed that. Thankfully, my mom's prognosis was good and after completing her chemotherapy she was pronounced cancer-free. She did not need to endure the radiation treatments and we were thankful for that.

Meanwhile, Jim continued to show improvement. About a year later we were told he could stop treatments because he appeared to be cancer-free. We were beyond delighted, only to have our celebration cut short when the doctor told us Jim could remain cancer-free for about two years. What? After all of this? I was under the illusion that cancer-free meant the battle had been won. The doctor explained that his type of cancer which was myxoid lipo sarcoma, always strikes back. He said, "Sarcomas come back with a vengeance."

About two years to the day the doctor made that prediction, Jim's cancer returned. We were told this time that the cancer was inoperable because to do so would require the removal of Jim's diaphragm. He would require a ventilator and the remaining cancer cells would continue to spread. Jesus!!! Is there no end to this shit!

I learned about hospice care which would allow Jim to die at home. We set up a hospital bed in the living room to prepare for the inevitable. Jim died at home September 18, 1988. He was just thirty-four years old. My children were seven, eight, fourteen and sixteen years old. Jeremy was one of his father's pall bearers.

I spent the days after Jim's death not wanting to leave my house. The days turned into weeks and my energy plummeted. It was a struggle just to get out of my bed. I found that writing in my journal, that I started when Jim was first diagnosed with cancer, helped me cope. I had named the story, "One Man's Battle," when I started writing about our fight against Jim's brutal cancer. I wrote about our ups and downs and talked about how the children adapted to our new normal. I called the final entry, "The Battle Was Lost," and with that, I closed that chapter of my life.

My caring neighbors left dinner casseroles on my porch, for which I was eternally grateful. I couldn't bring myself to shop for groceries yet. I knew the children needed to return to some form of normality, but I felt like a robot. It took a while for me to accept being a widowed single mom with four young children when I was just thirty-four years old. Eventually I did.

ENTER RANDY

In January 1989 I received an invitation to a surprise birthday party for my husband's hospice worker, Kate, in the mail. I casually tossed it aside along with a few pieces of junk mail. Lisa found the invitation as she sifted through some mail-order catalogs and insisted that I go to the party. She said she would take care of her little sisters so I could get out and do something fun. She rummaged through my closet and pulled out my cream-colored dress with a delicate floral pattern for me to wear. On the night of the party, Lisa insisted on applying my eye makeup, which I hadn't worn for ages, and then she combed and sprayed my short wispy blond hair. I remained apprehensive, saying maybe I should just stay home with the kids as she literally pushed me out the front door, tossing my car keys behind me, yelling, "Have fun!" I jumped into my car to escape the cold winter wind and drove off to the party.

Kate's house was only a short drive away and I figured I'd check out the party, say hello and leave. I hadn't been out socially in many years and really wasn't sure what to expect or even how to act at a party. I parked my black Ford Taurus along the curb a short distance away from Kate's house. As I walked toward her house, my new black leather boots kicked the freshly fallen January snow aside and it glistened. It was nice to be out, away from my daily responsibilities for a while. I climbed the steps leading up to Kate's porch. A cold brisk wind blew across my face as I rang the doorbell next to the ornate double doors embellishing the front of her beautiful home. Kate's husband, Mitch, opened the doors and seemed delighted to see me. He offered to take my heavy woolen coat and scarf and I entered the spacious living room full of guests. I scanned the group and realized I didn't know anyone there. My eyes were drawn to a large, silver half keg of draft beer in the kitchen. Ah, liquid courage! I helped myself to a cold draft beer and decided I was going to try to enjoy the festivities.

Suddenly, someone dimmed the lights in the living room signaling everyone to find a place to hide as Kate approached the regal Tuscany doors leading into the foyer. As she entered the living room, muffled giggling could be heard throughout the house. Kate reached for a nearby light switch and everyone sprang from their hiding places shouting "Surprise!" Mitch captured Kate's startled look and the smiling, happy partygoers on his video camera. It was apparent that Kate was truly surprised, which added to the fun.

I put a handful of crinkled potato chips and French onion dipping sauce on a heavyweight Dixie Paper Plate and casually headed back to the silver half keg to dispense a second robust porter draft beer. A tall, skinny guy approached me and offered to help me with the keg dispenser. He said, "Hi, I'm Randy, Kate's brother." I replied, "That's nice," as I proceeded to fill my glass after which I headed over to sit in front of the rustic stone fireplace to watch Kate open her presents. Randy followed me and asked if he could join me on the smooth hearth extension in front of the fireplace. I slid over and made a spot for him and we watched Kate open her birthday gifts. It was her fortieth birthday and everyone gave her gag gifts like coffee cups inscribed with "Over the Hill." I was laughing and having a good time.

Randy and I talked to each other like we were old friends. The hours seemed to fly by as we shared stories about our lives including our kids, pets and hobbies. I learned that he had two daughters from his previous marriage which ended in divorce. I was impressed to hear how Randy fought for joint custody of his girls so he would have more time to spend with them. I could see he was a good father who cared deeply about his girls and I felt this was an indication of his good character. He told me that his ex-wife died in a fiery automobile accident shortly after their divorce and he became a single father when they were still quite young. That had been a while ago and the girls were now in college. I told him about my four children and how they gave me reason to persevere through my husband's six-year battle with cancer that took his life just several months prior, making me a single mom.

CHAPTER 8

To lighten the conversation, Randy asked if I wanted
to try some of the fancy hors d'oeuvres which were laid out
on a long buffet table that was draped with a fancy white
lace table cloth. I spotted a chocolate fondue fountain with
tiers creating a magnificent "waterfall" of rich dark melted
chocolate. There was a white china platter full of luscious
red strawberries complete with fondue sticks to dip into the
chocolate. I found this irresistible. I used a Dixie paper plate
to gather a few strawberries that I smothered with chocolate
as Randy collected various hors d'oeuvres. We made our way
back to the fireplace and settled down to enjoy our feast. I
felt a calm, comfortable confidence that I hadn't experienced
since before Jim's cancer diagnosis.

I shared with Randy stories about most of my family
and where I was from. He told me he went to Catholic
University where he obtained his Electrical Engineering
degree. I replied that I had suffered through twelve years
of Catholic schooling and considered myself a recovering
Catholic. Eventually, I brought up my high school years at
Keough and shared how I was sexually abused by a perverted

priest named Father Maskell. Secretly, I thought that if the sexual abuse stories didn't send Randy running for the hills, I may have found an understanding friend. I talked about how I had a lot of pent-up anxiety and break-through memories about my abuse, especially over the past few years while my husband was undergoing all types of cancer treatments. I explained how I alternated between thinking about the cancer eating him up and Maskell abusing me in his office back in high school. Although Randy appeared shocked at times, he continued to listen, almost in awe.

Randy was open about his life as well. He told me it was tough for him growing up after his dad had a heart attack and died shortly before his twelfth birthday. I told him his sister Kate had been assigned as my deceased husbands hospice worker since she lost her dad when she was seven and my children were so young when Jim died. Hospice thought Kate would be a good match for my family because she could relate to losing a father at such a young age. I told him that Kate spoke about a brother getting injured in Vietnam when she was visiting during my husband's hospice care. I asked if he was the brother she spoke of. When he told me he was, assuming he was drafted, I expressed sorrow for him being forced to go to that god-forsaken place called Vietnam. Much to my surprise, Randy told me he volunteered. Initially, I was really shocked and I told him I had protested against that war along with all my hippie friends back in the day. I added that most of my friends had feared being drafted and even said they would flee to Canada before agreeing to be cannon fodder in the jungles of Vietnam.... for 'The Establishment.'

Randy, being the electrical engineer he is, explained his reasoning for volunteering. He told me that he learned how the military had to make sure that the operation of many different devices that used the electric spectrum could function near each other. These devices must be controlled to provide constant communication or radar data. Lives depend on that and maintaining communication without interference or radars without poor data was a very difficult task in combat areas. Radio Frequency Interference (RFI) as it is called, hurts electromagnetic compatibility (EMC) between all emitters thus reducing the chance of good results of movements, combat, or aid. Ok, I'm lost, I replied. I followed the part about lives depending on constant communication, but the stuff about the RFI's hurting the EMC's seemed a bit complex.

Randy explained that when he heard about the many RFI problems in Vietnam, as a graduate of Reserved Officers Training Course (ROTC), he volunteered for a six-month Vietnam assignment and entered the service as a 2nd lieutenant in the Air Force. I replied that it was a good thing he didn't have to join as a lowly private destined for the jungles. Randy agreed and added that as an officer, he was supposed to work in downtown Saigon on the RFI problems. He felt he would be safe there while staying in a hotel on Tudo Street in Saigon that was guarded by Vietnamese police. It was his understanding that while he was there, he would leave the hotel each morning and walk about half a block down Tudo Street to an American bus stop that would take him to work. That seemed simple enough.

Randy continued his story telling me how on one bright sunny day as he walked toward the bus stop with a sergeant, a claymore mine exploded from the left. The side blast lifted both of them off the walkway, carried them about fifteen feet into Tudo Street and dropped them on the concrete curb. Exploding shrapnel tore the sergeant's stomach open and he barely survived his injuries. Randy was knocked unconscious when his head hit the curb causing a concussion. His left leg was ripped open and bleeding as it was riddled with shrapnel. Remarkably, an address book that Randy carried in his left pants pocket prevented three additional pieces of shrapnel from piercing his upper thigh. He sustained permanent hearing loss in both ears as well. Overall, he considered himself very lucky not to be blown into many pieces. Randy learned later that a Navy Signalman about ten feet ahead of him was killed in the blast. I told him I was glad he survived that awful ordeal.

Kate came over and said, "I see you met my brother, Randy." She seemed irritated that I was spending the entire evening with her brother. I laughed because she told me after Jim had died that she wanted to introduce me to a lawyer friend of hers. I had previously told her I wanted to be a lawyer. She blurted out that there was a lawyer friend of hers there at her party that she wanted me to meet. She pointed to the buffet table, where he was standing. I glanced over at him and saw that he was short, fat and bald, not that it would have mattered to me, but I wasn't interested in talking to the lawyer. I looked at Kate and said, "I never said I wanted to meet a lawyer, I said I always wanted to *be* a lawyer." I told her that I chose to stay with Randy by the fireplace and share the many things we seemed to have in common. She was a bit disappointed because she was used to controlling things. Apparently, Kate had a single friend whom she had planned to hook up with Randy and she was a guest at the party.

Kate called me the next morning to thank me for coming to her party. She laughed as she told me that her brother asked her for my phone number. She said that her brother had fallen hard for me and wanted to date me. She added that she believed she had a duty to make sure things weren't moving too fast for me, considering the recent death of my husband. Wow! I hadn't dated anyone for more than sixteen years. I enjoyed talking to Randy at Kate's party, but did I want to get involved with him? My husband died just a few months ago. What would people think if I started dating so soon? Hell, I thought, it isn't the dark ages and women don't wear black to mourn for months and months anymore. Throwing caution to the wind, I told Kate to give her brother my number.

Randy called me later that week and we picked up where we left off. We talked like we had known each other forever. One thing led to another and Randy and I started dating exclusively. We started including my younger children in trips like visiting the Washington Arboretum and the nostalgic local drive-in movies. Once they got to know him, my daughters told me Randy was ok, which made me feel good about seeing him romantically. Several months later Randy moved from his home in Annapolis to be with me in Ellicott City. He brought his black cat, Inky, with him and both he and Inky became part of the family.

REMISSION DOESN'T MEAN YOU BEAT IT

In 1992 my mom's cancer appeared to come back, this time as ovarian cancer. The doctor recommended my mom undergo a biopsy of her ovary to determine whether she did in fact have ovarian cancer – he wasn't certain it was malignant. During the biopsy the lead surgeon allowed an intern to practise separating scar tissue from normal intestine tissue, while they were taking a sample of her ovary to be analyzed. This was never supposed to happen. My mom had harmless scar tissue from a prior diverticulitis infection and had had no problems with it.

Nevertheless, when the intern attempted to separate some of the scar tissue, he perforated my mom's intestine. Mom seemed fine after the biopsy and was supposed to go home the next day. Instead, her condition declined and her IV medication was increased which caused a fluid overload. The intern administered a drug called Lasix which was supposed to get rid of the excess fluid that had begun to affect her heart. Mom was rushed to intensive care where one mistake after another was made by incompetent doctors. My mother died of sepsis twenty-eight days later. It had started when the intern performed the unnecessary procedure and perforated her bowel, which caused harmful bacteria to leak into her abdomen. Her biopsy came back negative for ovarian cancer. All of this misery had been totally unnecessary.

The loss of my mom on February 13, 1993, continues to be the single most devastating event in my entire life. Words cannot describe how utterly lost I was during this time nor how much I miss her still. I didn't want to go on. I knew I had many responsibilities and that my children needed me desperately, but I was weary. I was so very tired of putting on the brave face and continuing to battle the "slings and arrows" of life. Fuck this!

I allowed myself to wallow in self-pity for several long weeks. I kept going over things in my head. How could I have saved my mom. The doctors' negligence is what finally killed her. I looked into my mom's past health problems. She had battled breast cancer ten years prior, underwent a radical mastectomy and had been pronounced cancer free for ten years. Why now, did the doctors suspect she had ovarian cancer? Why did she have to succumb to a needless botched biopsy?

With the help of my mom's medical records and personal notes about our family history, I was able to put together an alarming genetic picture of the high instances of both breast and ovarian cancers which had occurred on the maternal side of my family. A great aunt, my mom, two aunts, and at least two cousins had all been stricken with one or both of these cancers. There had to be a genetic connection.

My research led me to discover many new genetic tests that had recently become available. These help determine whether an individual possesses a genetic predisposition for a specific gene disorder. Human beings have a total of forty-six chromosomes comprised of twenty-three chromosomes inherited from each parent paired together within our DNA. Thousands of genes are located on each chromosome, and these genes may reveal potentially dangerous genetic mutations. An estimated 30,000 genes exist along the twenty-three pairs of chromosomes and function to repair damage and regulate the body. Interestingly this is merely a third more genes than the lowly round worm. Additionally, we also share versions of about ninety-eight percent of our genes with mice. Thus, it is not how much genetic material we have, but how it affects our growth, that is important.

The Human Genome Project examines the specific genetic material located in a chromosome called a "genome." Decoding the human genome enables scientists working on this project to understand the functions of each gene and how these genes coordinate each function. Thus, the manner in which an abnormal gene mutation causes a genetic disease may be determined. (Weiss, Rick, Life's Blueprint in Less Than an Inch; Research: Little of Genome Makes a Human, Wash. Post, Feb 11, 2001 at A1.)

The advancements made in The Human Genome project led to genetic testing designed to detect the genetic variations (called Alleles), which predispose individuals to specific genetic disorders such as Huntington's Disease (HD), Sickle-Cell Anemia, Breast/Ovarian Cancer and Cystic Fibrosis. After the gene mutation is located, an epidemiologist determines the statistical connection that the specific defective genetic profile has, with the manifestation of a genetic disorder. (Diver, Colin, S., Heimbold, Charles, A., Jr., & Cohen, Maslow, Jane, Point/Counterpoint: Genophia: What's Wrong With Genetic Predisposition? 149, U. Pa. L. Rev. 2001 at 1439.) Persons with a predisposition to a genetic disorder may seek the benefits of preventive treatment and advanced drug intervention now available for certain inherited disorders.

I decided to be proactive in my health care and underwent a genetic test at the Johns Hopkins Genetic Testing Center. Much to my dismay, I tested positive for the BRCAI mutation which predisposes me to both breast and ovarian cancers. At least I was finding answers. I was advised by genetic counselors that given my strong family history of breast and ovarian cancers, coupled with my newly discovered BRCAI mutation, I had about a ninety-four percent chance of contracting breast cancer by age sixty-four, and about a seventy percent chance of contracting ovarian cancer, during that time period. I considered this knowledge self-powering and elected to use enhanced monitoring through yearly mammograms and attempted to get on with my life.

THE ANONYMOUS LETTER

I continued to struggle with the horrible and shocking way my mom had died. My children were also suffering from the loss of their beloved grandmom so soon after losing their own Father. Randy did his best to support me and help cheer up the kids. I felt like a zombie going through the motions of life. Once again, I experienced intruding memories of Maskell and the horrific things he had done to me at Keough.

One morning I went to retrieve the mail. I found a strange anonymous letter asking if I knew of any improper behavior of a sexual nature that was going on at Keough during the years I was there. I was flooded with emotions of fear and relief as I read the letter. I ran around my back-yard laughing, crying and cursing. Maybe I wasn't crazy! There must be others out there that knew about Maskell! The letter included a phone number to call if I had information to share. You better believe I wanted to share what I knew about Maskell and the Keough abuse!

When I went to call the number in the anonymous letter, I felt paranoid. I was afraid to call from my house phone. Could it be traced? Who were these people who wanted to know about sexual misconduct at Keough?

Why now? I decided to find a phone booth in the next county, miles away from my house. I called the number on the letter. A female voice answered the phone. I asked her what she wanted to know about Keough. Did she want to know who was involved? She replied, "Well, why don't you tell me." I blurted out, "Father Maskell is a pervert and he sexually abused me at Keough." She told me her name was Beverly Wallace and that she was an attorney looking into reports of misconduct of a sexual nature at Keough.

Beverly told me she was working with two other lawyers, Phil Dantes and Jim Maggio at the law firm of Bragel, Kerr, Davis and Dantes in Towson, Maryland. She wanted to know if I would meet her at the firm to discuss the improper behavior I witnessed while I was a student at Keough. I agreed immediately.

Beverly, Phil and Jim introduced themselves and we started to talk about the anonymous letter as well as the newspaper inquiry they had mailed out to Keough alumni.

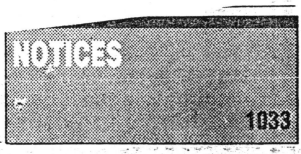

ANYONE WITH INFORMATION concerning any improprieties of a sexual nature involving faculty or other staff of the Archbishop Keough High School during the years 1968-1975, please contact us at PO Box 5438, Towson, MD 21285-5438.

I asked Beverly if there were any other alumnae from Keough who had contacted her to report sexual misconduct there. She informed me that there was another Keough alumna, whom they already represented. That woman was in the process of filing a lawsuit against Maskell, Keough and others under the name Jane Doe, for abuse she had experienced. Phil asked me if I would come forward as a witness for this woman since I seemed to know a lot about the abuse that went on at Keough. I did not know who this other woman was, but I said I would do anything in my power to expose Maskell and reveal what he did to me if it would help their client.

Once I understood there was another victim who had come forward, I disclosed everything I remembered about Maskell. I told them how I went to Maskell for help with a communication breakdown between my parents and me. I revealed how he took off all my clothes within the first fifteen minutes of meeting me in his office. I told them about the douches and the enemas that Maskell liked to administer to me. I did not know who Jane Doe was, but her courage to come forward made me confident to do the same. I finally found my voice.

Thoughts of Maskell consumed my days. I couldn't stop thinking about him and what he did to me. I experienced problems sleeping and one night I woke up screaming, "I was raped! They raped me!" Randy jumped out of bed looking for an intruder. I cried, "No, no, it was Maskell. He raped me." Randy tried to calm me down as I told him I remembered

Maskell and his friends raping me. He gave me the support I needed to get through this.

I called Beverley in the morning and she asked me to meet her at the office with her co-counsel Jim and Phil. I told her that I was remembering horrible things that Maskell did to me. I told her I felt like I was losing my mind. Jim Maggio asked me if I had ever sought psychological help after going through everything that happened to me. He asked me how I was able to go about day to day living with everything that happened to me. I told him that I wasn't really sure. Beverly suggested I talk to a psychologist, and gave me the name of one she knew and trusted. I made an appointment and started therapy for the first time since Keough.

I met with Beverly several weeks later and I told her I wanted to sue Maskell too. I told her I wanted to sue the church, the nuns, everybody responsible for what happened when I was at Keough, but I was afraid to use my real name. She explained that as a victim of rape, I could remain anonymous and I could join Jane Doe's lawsuit as a co-plaintiff. I would be Jane Roe.

CHAPTER 9

I AM JANE ROE

TELLING DAD

I knew I had to tell my dad about Maskell and my impending lawsuit before he read about the case in the local Baltimore Sun paper. I was overwhelmed with fear and sadness knowing I had to reveal my darkest secrets to him, after being a keeper of them for twenty-three years. How could I talk about it to him, decades after I left Keough and so soon after my mom's death? I always tried to cheer my dad up, and now I was about to tell him the unthinkable, vile things that a priest did to me. A priest my father held right up there with God. But it was time for my dad to know the truth.

That day, I reached into the depths of my soul and began to talk to my dad about Keough and what Maskell had done. I finally found the courage to reveal to him that Maskell touched me in a way he should not have. I told my dad that Maskell did sexual things to me, ordering me not to tell anyone or he would hurt me. I told him I was not the only girl Maskell raped, that I had found out about another girl he abused who was filing a lawsuit against Maskell and the Catholic Church. I told him I was joining the lawsuit as a co-plaintiff, Jane Roe. I felt like I was going to vomit, but I kept disclosing the things that went on in Maskell's office. Dad was horrified, shocked, and devastated and so very sorry to hear about the things Maskell did to me all those years ago.

Dad thought like the lawyer he was and rallied behind me. He told me he would do anything in his power to support me in my lawsuit. His legal mind took over and he saw my situation as a grave injustice, one that had to be dealt with. My dad never questioned anything I told him. He was worried about me and wanted me to know that it would be extremely difficult to get past the Statute of Limitations, which the opposition would argue had long passed. He wanted to make sure I felt strong enough to proceed. I assured him I was.

We were going up against a giant. Our confrontation paralleled the biblical story of David and Goliath where the small shepherd boy David sought to destroy the menacing giant Goliath with just a slingshot and a stone. This was going to be the fight of all fights. There really is not any way to prepare for something like this. How would the public react? Would I be believed? Would everyone view me as a nut job? Regardless, I saw the lawsuit as a way for me to finally tell my story, to reveal to everyone what Father Maskell had done to me at Archbishop Keough High School.

I was not yet an attorney. I did not fully understand the intricacies of launching a lawsuit, but I knew my case hinged on beating the Statute of Limitations (SOL).

THE STATUTE OF LIMITATIONS (SOL) EXPLAINED

The SOL is a prescriptive period of time after an event, within which a legal proceeding may be started. When the time specified in the SOL passes, a legal claim may no longer be filed. If such a claim is filed, it may be dismissed if the defense shows the claim is time-barred because it was filed after the SOL time period. The intentions of these laws are to facilitate resolution within a "reasonable" length of time. What amount of time is considered "reasonable" varies.

Under the SOL, I had three years from the time I reached the age of majority (eighteen) to sue Maskell and the Church for the sexual abuse I endured as a minor while attending Keough. This meant that I had until my twenty-first birthday to file a claim against Maskell, the Church and anyone else involved. I was forty at the time the Doe/Roe suit was filed.

However, I experienced new memories of my abuse shortly after my mom's untimely death in 1993. I found that when I focused on the details of what Maskell did to me, how he removed all of my clothes, how he inserted things into my vagina and into my anus, how I was repeatedly raped, new intruding memories surfaced. These new recovered or repressed memories were the basis of my lawsuit. As I understood it, my lawyers would argue that the SOL should run based on my recently recovered memories in 1994, which were well within the three-year prescriptive period.

REPRESSED MEMORY: ANOTHER HURDLE

What is repressed memory (also known as recovered memory and more recently dissociative amnesia)? Repression is a mechanism for avoiding conscious access to conflict-related material. The Diagnostic and Statistical Manual of Mental Disorders "DSM", which serves as the principal authority for psychiatric diagnoses, defines repressed memory as an "inability to recall autobiographical information." It states that "this amnesia may be localized (an event or period of time) or generalized (identity or life history.)" A person often copes with severe trauma by dissociating from what is happening. This detachment can block the memory of the event as a means of survival.

Often during my abuse, I felt as though I wasn't present in my body, like I was a spectator watching myself being raped. There were many things I could not remember, such as how I got dressed after Maskell took off all my clothes. I started to experience new intruding thoughts relating to my abuse around the time I lost my mom. As time went on, I remembered multiple rapes that occurred during my abuse at Keough. It was these rapes that formed the foundation of my lawsuit.

The church's defense lawyers would seek to discredit repressed memory as a falsehood. To make matters worse during the early 1990's, the term "False Memory Syndrome" (FMS), a non-psychological term, was used by defense lawyers to dispute repressed memory. False Memory Syndrome is a fabrication originated by a private foundation whose stated purpose was to support parents accused of sexually abusing their children. In Doe/Roe, the defense brought in FMS expert Paul McHugh to testify that I was suffering from FMS. FMS has NOT been recognized in the DSM. Today cases involving repressed memory continue to hinge on the Battle of the Experts, meaning that the two opposing sides introduce expert witnesses to submit contradictory testimonies in an attempt to sway the Judge and jury to decide in their favor.

THE COMPLAINT

The Complaint is a legal document that details the facts that support the claim that the plaintiff's legal rights were violated. My Complaint was filed against:

A. Joseph Maskell,

B. Dr. Christian Richter,

C. the School Sisters of Notre Dame,

D. Seton Keough High School,

E. the Archdiocese of Baltimore,

F. Archbishop William Keeler Roman Catholic Archbishop of Baltimore and his Predecessors and Successors in the Circuit Court of Baltimore City in Towson, Maryland on August 29, 1994. So began the Doe/Roe v A. Joseph Maskell, et. al. lawsuit.

THESE THINGS TAKE TIME

A typical lawsuit can take anywhere from one to three years to settle, depending on whether the defendant is willing to settle the case before it proceeds to trial. Most defendants are willing to make an out-of-court settlement offer because it is very expensive to go to trial. Of course, the AOB was unlikely to offer to settle. Given the amount of material we had to cover in the Doe/Roe case, I fully expected it to take much longer than the three-year average. The stress of my impending trial was heavy. I tried to deal with the almost constant pressure, by continuing actively to involve myself with my family.

Life continued while I awaited the next phase of my lawsuit against Maskell and the church. I was forty years old, taking care of four kids, trying to get my college degree, all while in the middle of the Doe/Roe lawsuit. I continued taking courses at the local Catonsville Community College, where I was studying to be a Social Worker. I had to take a break, however, and seek medical care because I started experiencing severe abdominal pain. I soon learned I had endometriosis which causes tissue that normally lines the uterus, to grow outside the uterine wall and into the ovaries, the fallopian tubes, and the tissue lining the pelvis. My gynecologist, Dr. Pat Mosser, advised me to undergo a hysterectomy, given the fact that I had an extremely painful case of endometriosis, my strong family history of both breast and ovarian cancer, and my BRCAI Gene Mutation, that put me at very high risk for contracting ovarian cancer.

My doctor further advised that I undergo a laparoscopic hysterectomy, considered the least invasive. She explained how the laparoscope is inserted through two tiny incisions at the site of each ovary to help locate them and an additional small incision is made at the naval for another guiding scope. The uterus, ovaries and Fallopian tubes are removed through the vagina (birth canal) so there is no need to make an incision across the abdomen. Dr. Mosser added that I would be able to leave the hospital the day after the procedure. It all sounded like a well calculated plan, but I was apprehensive and the doctor noted my hesitation. She said that given my medical history, if I elected not to undergo the hysterectomy, she strongly suggested I enter an ovarian cancer monitoring group. These kinds of cancers are typically not found until they are well advanced and it is too late. This scared me.

Two things troubled me. I was concerned about complications and excessive bleeding because I have a hereditary condition called Ehlers Danlos Syndrome (EDS).

This can cause greater bleeding during surgical procedures. EDS is basically a collagen disorder that causes the skin to be more fragile. I told Dr. Mosser I had been diagnosed with EDS years earlier when I first learned that my children had the disorder. She insisted that I would not have a problem with the vaginal removal, because I had had four children and my vagina was malleable. She then rubbed the skin on the back of my hand and said, "Quite frankly I don't see any significant sign of Ehlers Danlos with you."

I told Dr. Mosser that I was going to consult with my geneticist who was also an EDS specialist, before we set a date for the surgery. My geneticist, Dr. Alice Horn, instructed me to make sure that my surgeon was aware of the potential complications that could occur after surgery in EDS patients. Overall, she believed that since I had a milder form of EDS, I should be OK with the laparoscopic hysterectomy.

WHAT EXACTLY IS EDS

Ehlers-Danlos syndrome was named after the two doctors, Edvard Ehlers and Henri-Alexandre Danlos who first described this disorder. It is a collagen deficiency caused by a mutation in a group of approximately twenty genes. Collagen is connective tissue that strengthens our skin, bones, blood vessels, and joints. It is the 'glue' that holds us together. Some types of EDS involve blood vessels and internal organs and can be deadly, while other types that involve the skin and joints mainly cause extreme elasticity and flexibility. Because of this elasticity, joints can become easily dislocated. The prognosis depends on the 'type' of EDS a person has. I was told I carried the classical type of EDS which is a milder form, but I have experienced various joint problems throughout my life that have been linked to the disorder.

Many people go through their entire lives not knowing they have EDS. It is often misdiagnosed as a psychiatric problem, chronic fatigue syndrome or even depression. I often describe EDS by giving examples of famous people who have the disorder. For example, Gary Turner, who has a more serious form of EDS, was a circus sideshow performer who holds the Guinness World Record for the most elastic skin. Also, although it was never definitively proven by a skin biopsy, the famous escape artist, Harry Houdini, is suspected of having had EDS. His extreme joint flexibly which enabled him to dislocate and relocate his joints to escape a straitjacket during his performances, could be attributed to a form of EDS.

My second concern about the hysterectomy surfaced after I read the consent/release form I was required to sign prior to the surgery. It stated that if I contracted ovarian cancer from a part of the ovarian tissue inadvertently left inside me, I would not hold Dr. Mosser or the hospital responsible. After reading about this possibility, I told my doctor that I would prefer the traditional hysterectomy with an abdominal incision where all the organs would be totally visible since the main goal was to make sure all the tissue was removed. Again, she assured me that I had nothing to worry about and that she would get all the tissue out. So, I signed the release.

Randy took me to the hospital for my procedure and things seemed to go well initially. Even though I was experiencing a lot of post-op pain, and abdominal swelling, Dr. Mosser signed a release for me to leave the hospital. I was sent home with Tylenol 3 for the pain shortly after the surgery. Once home, I started vomiting every half hour and my level of pain increased greatly. I then developed a fever and had to be rushed back to the hospital.

Upon arrival at the emergency room, the attending physician ordered painful sonograms and x-rays while I vomited bile uncontrollably. They performed tests for over eight hours before finally admitting me. At that point, Dr. Mosser came in and told Randy that I had a paralyzed bowel, which would correct itself. She instructed a nurse to perform a nasogastric intubation, which is a procedure to insert a tube into the nose down into the stomach to drain off some of the bile collecting in the abdomen. After several more days of watching me vomit bile, Randy asked Dr. Mosser, "How many cases like this have you treated?" She replied, "One." Randy, seeing that I was in intense pain and still vomiting, told Dr. Mosser she was officially removed from my case.

We requested an examination by the hospital internist, who ordered more abdominal x-rays and a barium swallow test which revealed dilated loops of my small intestines, consistent with ileus, a painful obstruction of the ileum or other part of the intestine. Basically, I had a blockage in my small intestine that stopped the movement of any food or fluid through my digestive system and caused me to have excruciating pain. Additionally, a staple had been affixed to my greater omentum and had to be removed as soon as possible.

WHAT IS THE GREATER OMENTUM?

The greater omentum is a large apron-like membrane that forms the lining of the abdomen. It is supported by a thin layer of connective tissue and covers the lower portion of the stomach, small intestines, colon and the posterior abdominal wall. It contains blood vessels, lymphatic vessels and nerves. The greater omentum is also known as *epiploon*, a Greek word that means 'to float on' and can appear to float over the intestines.

BACK TO THE OR

Fortunately, there was an abdominal surgeon on call whom I knew, Dr. Kevin McCabe, who had successfully operated on my mom several years back. She had an acute case of diverticulitis which required a bowel resection with primary anastomosis, which is the removal of infected colon and repair to reattach two healthy sides of the previous infection. I totally trusted Dr. McCabe and was relieved that he was taking over my case. Dr. McCabe told me that I did not have a paralyzed bowel. The only way to get me well was to operate immediately to remove an obstruction, which was preventing anything from moving through my intestines in a normal manner. I was extremely weak from all the pain and vomiting I had experienced over the past few days. I barely had the ability to comprehend how serious my situation had become.

As I went into the operating room, I was so convinced that I was going to die, I told the anesthesiologist I'd forgive him if he killed me. I warned him that he would be leaving my four children to face the world as orphans. Dramatic?

Yes, but at that point I was terrified. I remembered that when my brother Mark was in medical school, one of his professors told him that during surgeries the anesthesiologist was responsible for more deaths than any doctor or nurse. This statement was embedded in my mind as I entered the operating room. Of course, nowadays anesthesia is considered very safe because doctors have extensive knowledge of the anesthetic drugs and the quality of anesthetic care, is stellar. There are few perioperative adverse outcomes such as coma or death related directly to anesthesia today. Nevertheless, at the time of my emergency surgery, I spoke up and startled my anesthesiologist.

NEAR DEATH EXPERIENCE

While I was under the anesthesia, I remembered being in a very bright, small but pleasant room listening to my Mom talk to me. Her voice appeared to be coming from a hole in the wall opposite from where I was sitting. I was so happy to hear her sweet voice! She told me that I was going to be OK and that my work on earth was not nearly finished.

As she spoke these words, I kept trying to make my way to where her voice was. I touched the wall which was very pliable, almost like rubber. I told Mom that I wanted to stay with her, that I didn't want to go back. She told me I had to go back to the children who needed me and that I had other important work to do. At that moment I tried to grab onto the opening in the wall so I could jump through the hole to be with her. I guess my Mom knew what I was trying to do because suddenly I heard her yell "Go back," and the hole snapped shut. My eyes sprang open to see Randy looking down at me. He was crying, saying I was going to be OK. I felt great sadness and told him I just wanted to stay with my Mom. It took me about three months to fully recover from my ordeal and to feel strong enough to continue my battle against the Church.

THE DISCOVERY PHASE/YOU WON'T
BREAK ME

It wasn't easy to pretend I was normal while the Doe/Roe lawsuit loomed. Shortly after my medical ordeal we entered the discovery phase of my case. "Discovery" is the term used to describe the legal tools lawyers use to reveal facts pertinent to the claims and defenses at issue in a lawsuit. The discovery process allows both sides in a lawsuit to adequately prepare for trial and avoid surprises which can undermine the outcome. Depositions are part of the discovery process; the defense has the right to ask the plaintiff questions related to the lawsuit. These questions are asked in person.

The following defense attorneys were present at my depositions: J. Michael Lehane - Counsel for Maskell; Kevin Murphy - Counsel for Archdiocese; Shirlie Norris Lake - Counsel for Richter; T. Rogers Harrison - Counsel for School Sisters of Notre Dame.

These attorneys respectively took turns asking me many questions over a period of six days. Each deposition session started around 9:30 a.m., broke for lunch, and resumed around 1p.m. The queries were brutal and included questions about my character, thoughts, sexual history, family, and basically anything about me the defense lawyers wanted to explore. This was their chance to intimidate me, to make me feel small, to make me cry, to make me give up.

One of the lawyers, Ms. Lake asked questions in a calm tone as though she was my caring friend who was there to help me. She went back and forth interrogating me about my visits to Dr. Richter, whom she represented. The following account is taken exactly as it appears in the transcribed depositions on the record.

Q: Did he put a finger into your vagina?

A: Yes, yes, they both did (referring to Maskell and Richter)

Q: Did he touch you externally, or inside of your vagina?

A: It was external separation.

Q: But we are not talking about your legs now?

(from page 161 of depositions)

Q: When you couldn't see because of the sheet, why do you say that that was Father Maskell?

A: Because I could see and feel him moving around and doing something with his hands as I felt simultaneously, I could see Maskell.

(From page 162 of deposition)

More questions from Lawyer Lake:

Q: Okay. I'm still confused as to some of – these meetings or sessions that supposedly happened with Father Maskell. On one of those occasions, Linda Trescott was present?

A: Yes.

Q: Now, her being present at one of those occasions was something you've always remembered; isn't that correct?

A: Yes.

Q: And on that occasion, you were instructed to undress while Linda was instructed by Doctor Maskell—Father Maskell to touch and point out the various parts of your female anatomy, is that correct?

A: Yes.

Q: And did Father Maskell say, tell me what that is that you're touching, or did he ask Linda Trescott to touch it and tell him what she was touching?

A: I'm not sure how he worded it.

Q: Now, you've known, you've recalled and knew about that all along, isn't that correct?

A: Yes.

Q: And that's part of the information in addition to the suppositories, the enemas, and the douches that you've previously described that made up the information that led you to believe that Father Maskell was a pervert, is that correct?

A: Yes.

Q: And that incident was one of those things that you characterized as a perversion, isn't that correct?

A: Yes.

Q: Now, you knew when that was happening with you and Linda Trescott and Father Maskell that it was absolutely wrong; isn't that correct?

A: Yes.

Q: Inappropriate, immoral, wrong; isn't that correct?

A: Yes.

Q: Was that occasion that that happened with Linda Trescott your first or second session with Father Maskell?

A: It was after my first meeting with Father Maskell. I'm not sure which session it was. There were many sessions.

Q: Now your first session with Father Maskell, you also recall what happened at that session, isn't that correct?

A: Yes.

Q: And that was when you came to him to talk about your parents; is that correct?

A: Yes, that's correct.

Q: He had you undress; is that correct?

A: Yes.

Q: You sat naked on his lap; is that correct?

A: Yes.

Similar questions followed and the attorney asked why I didn't refuse to go back to Maskell. As if I had a choice....

Another lawyer, Mr. Harrison, questioned me as though I were a disgusting liar seeking to get rich off the nuns he represented. At one point I answered one of his questions with, "If you would ask me the question like a human being, I would gladly answer it." He retorted, "Strike that from the record." To which I replied that I did not think he was human. Part of Deposition by Harrison:

Q: Well, to me you got external and you got internal. Did he perform an internal pelvic exam on you on your first visit? Yes or No?

A: No.

Q: And to the extent that anyone says you told them recently that Maskell performed an internal pelvic exam on you in the first visit, that person would be untruthful; isn't that correct?

A: No, they wouldn't because he touched me vaginally. He did not insert an instrument that a gynecologist uses. That's what I, I think of as an internal examination. He didn't use an instrument. He touched me, as you said, fondled me vaginally after the breast. So – he looked at my vagina, so we could say he performed a vaginal examination, but I wouldn't go as far to say an internal.

Q: Well, I guess that could be an explanation of what internal means, but did you – have you told anybody within the last two years that Father Maskell did an internal pelvic exam on you on your first visit to him?

A: Yes.

Q: And in fact, Doctor Maskell –

MS. WALLACE: Father.

Q: -- Father Maskell did do an internal pelvic exam on your first visit?

A: Yes.

Q: And the fact that Father Maskell did an internal pelvic exam on you on the first visit is something you've known ever since he did it; isn't that correct?

A: Yes.

Q: Now, you – I thought there was some confusion at the last deposition, it was probably on my part. There's no question that you know now and you have known all along that Father Maskell actually administered enemas to you; isn't that correct?

A: I knew that I had taken the enemas in his office. I knew he watched me, in the bathroom, but it was the Fall of '93 before I actually remembered him inserting the enema into my body.

Q: Anyone who would say that you previously stated within the last two years that Doctor – that Father Maskell himself administered an enema to you and that you've told them, that would not be truthful; is that correct?

A: No, that's not correct because he gave me the enema. I had to take them in his presence. And so, if they said he gave me enemas, they'd be truthful.

Q: So, to you, to administer an enema is the equivalent of him watching you give it to yourself, is that what you're telling me?

A: He made me take the enemas, and he, he – gave me a suppository that I remembered all along.

Q: We're not talking about suppositories right now. We're talking about an enema. Did you or did you not state within the last two years that you have known all along – is there something fascinating on Mr. Maggio's notes over there or something ma'am?

A: No, there's not.

Q: I was just curious.

MR. MAGGIO: Want to read my notes?

MR. HARRISON: Yeah, if you let me. I'd love to.

Q: (By Mr. Harrison) Have you stated within the last two years to anyone that Father Maskell administered, gave you an enema and that you've known that all along?

A: He gave me an enema. Yes, I stated he gave me the enema.

Q: The testimony that you had provided about the conversation back and forth between Maskell and Richter during the gynecological exam about, you know, launch pad and freight train and those topics, was that something that you've always, always remembered?

A: Yes.

Q: Did Father Maskell ever, based upon your new memory, did Father Maskell ever expose himself to you or force you to engage in any sexual activity with him?

A: Yes.

Q: Based upon your old memory, the memory you had all along, did Father Maskell ever expose himself to you or force you to engage in any type of sexual activity?

A: No

Q: What is sexual activity to you?

A: Intercourse.

Q: So, a priest performing an internal pelvic examination, fondling your breasts, inserting his finger in your vagina, you don't perceive those things to be sexual activity?

A: Now that you word it that way, yes, I suppose.

I felt revictimized during those depositions and found the continuing questioning painful. One of the Church lawyers asked me if all Maskell did was perform a gynecological exam on me, acting as my doctor? It was as if they were justifying his actions. I told them Maskell was not a doctor even though they often referred to him as Doctor Maskell instead of Father Maskell during the questioning. I also told them he liked to give me douches in his office bathroom when I was a Keough student. I tried my best not to be intimidated.

These lawyers (except Ms. Lake, who represented Dr. Richter) were hired guns, paid for by the corporate giant-- The Archdiocese of Baltimore (AOB), the Roman Catholic Church. Their job was to confuse, embarrass, and break me. My lawyers were there to shield me as best they could from being badgered and bullied by the opposition any more than legally permitted. A particularly demeaning session occurred when Mr. Murphy asked the following:

Q: "Do you foresee yourself doing a particular kind of job?"

A: "Yes, I want to be a lawyer."

A discussion off the record took place where they mocked me, acting as though I could never reach such a lofty goal. (From page 31 of depositions)

People were interested in our case. I agreed to talk with two investigative journalists, Robert A. Erlandson and Joe Nawrozki of The Baltimore Sun paper, as well as local TV news reporters about my case so that my side of the story got out there.

On several occasions I thought we were going to win our case. On August 10, 1994, I learned that the police found many mysterious boxes buried in a pit twelve feet square and ten feet deep at the Holy Cross Cemetery in South Baltimore. I learned that in 1990, when Maskell was pastor of Holy Cross Parish, he had the cemetery caretaker, William Storey, bury the mysterious boxes of records. In *The Keepers*, an anonymous police source, known as "Deep Throat," claimed that when the boxes were exhumed in 1994, they contained original photographs of girls with their breasts exposed and typed profiles of high school girls. Deep Throat went on to say there was enough evidence to arrest Maskell and stated, "We could have done it right then and there."

Surely, people would believe that Maskell abused me. Surely, the police will find enough evidence to convict

Maskell. I mean who buries a truck load of boxes full of God knows what, in a cemetery?

Conversely, State Attorney Sharon A.H. May maintained that there were no original photographs in the boxes and in *The Keepers* stated, "To my recollection there was nothing that went right to "Maskell molested these kids." However, she added, "Maybe we did [find pornographic material], I don't remember that."

At one point during the lawsuit, it was my understanding that one of the boxes contained information about me. The bottom line is I should have been permitted to view the material in that box, especially if it related to me in some way. Instead, some of the material was taken to Judge Caplin, who was presiding over the Doe/Roe case, for what is called an *in-camera* review.

WHAT IS AN 'IN-CAMERA' REVIEW

The term *in camera* is Latin for "in chambers." An *in-camera* review is typically an examination of evidence conducted in the privacy of the judge's chambers to determine whether it will be presented to the jury or made public. When a judge decides to conduct such a review, she hears discussion by both the plaintiff's attorneys and the defendant's attorneys as to why or why not certain evidence should be admitted. To my dismay, after performing an *in-camera* review, the judge in my case decided the material from the cemetery pit was inadmissible.

HOW MANY DID MASKELL ABUSE?

The anonymous letters that were sent out requesting information about sexual misdeeds at Keough, led to the discovery of more victims. My attorneys informed me that women from Keough were coming forward and supporting my account of Maskell as a predator priest. Some of these women reported that they too were abused by Maskell.

I could not wait until my lawyers deposed Maskell. I wanted to see how he would answer questions about his extensive sexual abuse ring at Keough. But that was never to happen. After Maskell was removed from ministry on July 31, 1994, he fled to Wexford, Ireland, where he was employed by the Irish Health and Safety Executive (HSE) as a counselor. He practiced psychology for about seven months there, according to the Irish national health agency. Subsequently, Maskell continued to work as a private psychologist in the area until 1998. All this time, he had access to children. Baltimore church officials have said they barred Maskell from public ministry in 1994 and that he went to Ireland without their knowledge. They said they were unaware of his whereabouts until 1996, when they learned he was living in Wexford. In 1999 he returned to America where he died two years later without ever facing charges for the sexual abuse.

Sadly, Maskell escaped justice and was never deposed during the Doe/Roe lawsuit. I never had the opportunity to watch him answer questions from my lawyers. He never had to sit in the "hot seat" while lawyers dug into every aspect of his life, as I did during my six days of brutal depositions. Moreover, the church never had to produce documents pertaining to the case or explain his mysterious trip to Ireland.

I knew there had to be written evidence of some of the things Maskell had done. I decided to search through some old boxes my dad had among his retired legal files that were stored in his home office. I uncovered relevant documents among my dad's files and found a letter dated October 9, 1970, from Maskell to Dr. Franklin Guzman (the psychiatrist) written on Keough stationary. The letter starts out stating, "Pursuant to our telephone conversation of yesterday I am writing to you to refer Teresa Fidelis Harris of our school to you for psychiatric evaluation and treatment." He goes on to say, "The problem which concerns me the most at present is to determine whether this young girl has developed a state of schizophrenia or not, and if so, how best to treat the situation. The underlying psychological state is a confused and mistrusting one which manifests itself in bizarre ways." In closing Maskell writes, "Please contact me in reference to your diagnosis and to advise how you feel this situation could best be met from our position both academically and in the counseling role." Wtf! This letter stunned me. No wonder my parents thought I was insane. Maskell had them right where he wanted them…in a state of fear for my life.

This letter was wrong on so many levels I didn't know where to begin to try to understand it. First, Maskell speaks as a doctor, which he was NOT, and he tells Dr. Guzman that I was in "a state of schizophrenia!" I'm not a doctor but I know you don't ever get a "state" of schizophrenia!! This is Maskell accusing me of being nuts when he was covering himself by making me look paranoid in case I ever TOLD on him. No one would ever believe a confused teen rather than a priest.

I also found Guzman's response to Maskell detailing his diagnosis of me: "I am placing her on Thorazine 10 mgs. B.I.D. for which a prescription was given. Her anxiety at the present time is great, but she is mainly depressed, lonely, and frightened." Surely, Maskell crossed a line by orchestrating my medical and psychological care. How I wished he could have been questioned in a courtroom about this. What qualified him to take control of my life so completely. How many other girls were being subjected to his evil ways?

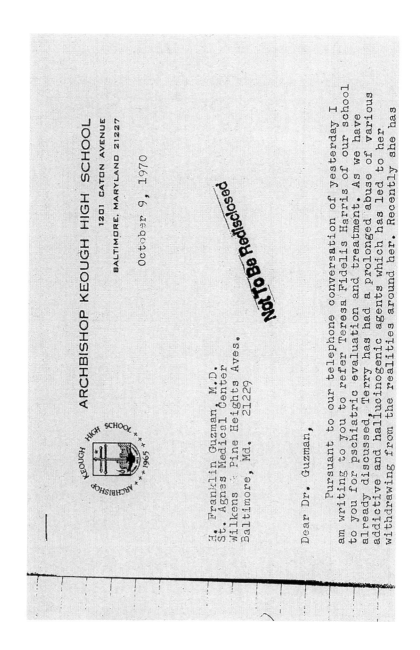

ARCHBISHOP KEOUGH HIGH SCHOOL

1201 CATON AVENUE

BALTIMORE, MARYLAND 21227

October 9, 1970

Not To Be Redisclosed

H. Franklin Guzman, M.D.
St. Agnes Medical Center
Wilkens & Pine Heights Aves.
Baltimore, Md.   21229

Dear Dr. Guzman,

Pursuant to our telephone conversation of yesterday I
am writing to you to refer Teresa Fidelis Harris of our school
to you for pschiatric evaluation and treatment. As we have
already discussed, Terry has had a prolonged abuse of various
addictive and hallucinogenic agents which has led to her
withdrawing from the realities around her. Recently she has

222

exhibited what appear to be recurrences of hallucinations from previous drug use and has acted in a somewhat paranoid manner towards those around her. She has also manifested definite suicidal tendencies. There is a strong animosity towards her parents which she apparently projects into their actions towards her. The problem which concerns me the most at present is to determine whether this young girl has developed a state of schizophrenia or not and, if so, how best to treat the situation. The underlying psychological state is a confused and mistrusting one which manifests itself in bizarre ways.

Enclosed please find copies of our academic record on Terry which contains the basic information on this girl. I will ask Terry's father, Mr. Joseph B. Harris, to contact you to set up a time for evaluation.

Please contact me in reference to your diagnosis and to advise us how you feel this situation could best be met from our position both academically and in the counselling role.

Thanking you for your consideration and help, I am,

Sincerely,

Rev. H. Joseph Maskell

NAME OF PATIENT: Teresa Harris.   DATE SEEN: October 10, 1970.

Not To Be Redisclosed

PSYCHIATRIC EVALUATION:

Teresa is a 16 years old white girl referred to me by Father Maskel, Chaplain, Archbishop Keoh High School. Her chief complaints were, depressed, loneliness and using drugs, marihuana, LSD, barbiturates and once she said she took a shot of morphine. Throughout the interview she was very guarded in telling me any of the symptoms or effects that some of the drugs will entice. Her reluctancy I found had no real basis and it makes me wonder whether she has actually had any experience at all. She was born in Baltimore, the youngest of 4 children and the only one in the family presenting any overt emotional problems. The three oldest ones are boys, one married and two in college ages 19 and 18. Terry has had the usual childhood diseases USD without any complications. Recently she visited a Gyn man for fear of being pregnant or having VD. This prooved to be incorrect and she said she feels better about it. She attended St. William's Parrish since age 6 getting straight A's and observing good behaviour. She is attending her Junior year at Keoh where her grades have been average but dropping within the past year. She relates well to her teachers both male and females. Her menarchia occured at age 13. She was fearful and disappointed not only because she did not know anything about it but because she had no one to turn to. Terry's parents are alive. Her impression of them is a negative one. She says that she feels a strange person in her own house. The only close attachment she has at the

224

present time is with her boyfriend whom she describes as caring for him but not loving him. This boy apparently is also having difficulties and is apparently involved in the use of drugs. Terry's present difficulties appear to stem out of a very deficient relationship with her parents, of a growing sense of responsibilities and her consequent inability to face these with any degree of support, enthusiasm and maturity. Her psychological make up reveals a frightened, confused adolescent whose normal weariness has turned into a nightmare. I feel that she is quite capable of dangerous acting out both outwardly and inwardly. Under stress she presents definite signs of borderline psychotic disorders but at the present time she is managing to appear rational and coherent. Her main defense mechanism and introjection, denial and she has been unable to sublimate at all. Terry may have a chance to understand her present difficulties and for this reason she will be seen on weekly therapeutic sessions and I am placing her on Thorazine 10 mgs. B.I.D. for which a prescription was given. Her anxiety at the present time is great but she is mainly depressed, lonely and frightened.

DIAGNOSTIC IMPRESSION: Adjustment reaction of adolescence, with depressive features.

H. Franklin Guzman, M.D.

HFG/malp

As if the correspondences between Maskell and Guzman weren't chilling enough, I found more letters from him written on his Keough stationary to his gynecologist buddy, Dr. Richter as well as Richter's letters responding to Maskell. In one such letter dated November 16, 1970, Richter writes, "This patient was seen at the request of the school councilor at Archbishop Keough High School because of a minor gynecological complaint and anxiety." (Note: the word "councilor" was misspelled in the doctor's letter.) Nothing was sacred; my medical records, the description of my "moderate" sized breasts, the prescription for Koremex douches, are included in these exchanges. No words.

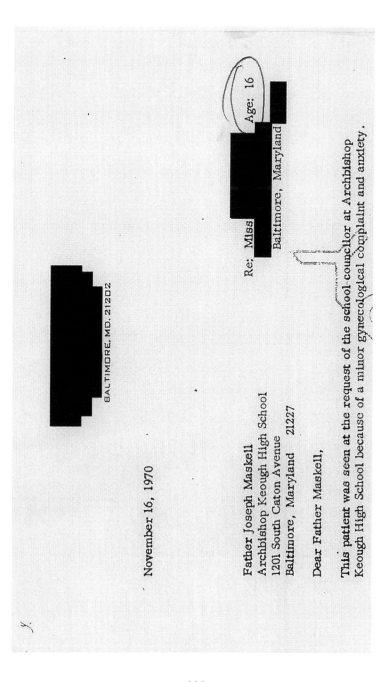

November 16, 1970

Re: Miss ███████

█████████
Baltimore, Maryland

Age: 16

Father Joseph Maskell
Archbishop Keough High School
1201 South Caton Avenue
Baltimore, Maryland   21227

Dear Father Maskell,

This patient was seen at the request of the school-councilor at Archbishop
Keough High School because of a minor gynecological complaint and anxiety.

██████ BALTIMORE, MD. 21202

The physical findings were within normal limits except for a minor gynecological problem which was treated medically. A follow up examination four weeks later revealed an improvement in the patient's gynecological condition; her mental attitude was also much improved. Miss ███ was advised in her physical activity at this time and told to continue visits with the school councilor.

My gratitude for this referral, and I also hope the patient will have a speedy return to normal.

Respectfully yours,

Terry Harris   Age: 16   Re: Father Joseph Maskell.
Archbishop Keough High School

500 Nottingham Road

Baltimore, Maryland 21229

10/7/70   Patient seen at request of Father Joseph Maskell for vaginal discharge. She has been on L.S.D., barbiturates and amphetamine. There are signs of mental withdrawel. Cycles irregular. Flow normal. No period for two months. Bowels and urinary function normal. Irritating vaginal discharge. Patient feels quilty.

Breasts: Moderate in size. No abnormal masses or secretions. No axillary masses.

Abdomen: Flat, No scars, hernia, masses or tenderness. L.K.&S. within normal limits.

Pelvic: Marital introitus. Some inflammation on skin of the labia. Vaginal mucosa inflammed. Moderate monitial like leucorrhoea. Uterus anterior position, normal size. Adnexae negative.

Rectal: Good tone. No masses.

IMPRESSION   1. Monilial vaginitis

RX:
1. Mycostatin supp.
2. Recheck two weeks

RICHTER

11/7/70   Wt: 116 1/2   L.M.P. 10/20/70   B.P. 120/80

P.I.   Discharge has receded – slight amount remains. Slight vaginal soreness. Recent constipation. Normal urinary function.

Abdomen: Small and flat. Slight tender. No masses palpable. L.K.&S. within normal limits.

Pelvic: Normal external genitalia. Vaginal mucosa and cervix clean. Thin watery Leukorrhea. Walls well supported. Uterus anterior position. Normal size. Both adnexae negative.

Rectal: Good tone. No masses.

IMPRESSION   No gyn. pathology

RX: 1. Advise exercise

231

HARRIS, Miss Terry

3/22/71   Vaginal itching and burning. Cycles about 42 days. Flow normal. Occasional intermenstrual spotting. Bowel and urinary function normal.

EXAM: L.M.P. 3/8/71   B.P. 130/80

Breasts: Moderate in size. No abnormal masses or secretions. No axillary masses.

Abdomen: Flat. No scars, glands, hernia, masses or tenderness. L.K.&S. not palpable.

Pelvic: Normal external genitalia. Slight inflammation of vulva. Small amount of leukorrhea. Uterus anterior position, normal size. Adnexae negative.

Rectal: Good tone. No masses.

IMPRESSION: Vulvitis

RX: 1. Urine negative S&A
       2. Koremex douche

Looking back at how I must have appeared as a high school girl in Keough, I can see how my mannerisms may have been perceived as "strange." After all, I had reason to be "depressed, lonely and frightened." A friend of mine, Anne, once told me that I had "a natural reaction to an unnatural action." Until people understand what was going on underneath the surface, they couldn't understand my teenage behavior resulting from the horrific acts of my abuser.

DEFENSE MOTION TO DISMISS

A Motion to Dismiss is a document filed with the court asking the judge to throw out certain claims in a civil or criminal case, or to throw out the case altogether. A Motion to Dismiss is often filed by a defendant immediately after the lawsuit has been served but may be filed at any time during the proceedings.

The defense in the Doe/Roe case filed a Motion to Dismiss or in the Alternation a Motion for Summary Judgement arguing that my:

1. Claim was Barred by the SOL

2. Evidence of PTSD With Amnesia and Testimony Based Upon Recovered Memories is Inadmissible and

3. Roe Was on Inquiry Notice of Her Potential Cause of Action

The Court set aside several days for a Hearing on these three issues. A hearing is a proceeding that takes place in front of the judge before the actual case is even presented. It is an opportunity for the defense to provide legal evidence why the case in question should be dismissed. Testimony is presented in the courtroom to support the evidence that the defense attorneys set forth. Our case had to survive a court hearing on the Motion to Dismiss before we could argue the actual case before a jury. The main issue was the defense's argument that the SOL had run and the time for me to sue had long passed. Additionally, they alleged that any new or recovered memories I had about being raped, did not prevent the SOL from taking effect because repressed memories could not be scientifically supported. The defense also argued that I possessed the sophistication to have filed a lawsuit by the time I was twenty-one years of age and I basically *slept on my legal right* and thus allowed the SOL pass.

THE COURT HEARING

Even though the hearing on the Motion to Dismiss is a preliminary matter and not the actual trial, it can be very intimidating to the plaintiffs giving testimony. In my case the judge made it known that we were not in court to prove or disprove the allegations of sexual abuse. We were there to determine whether or not the SOL prevented the case from going forward. We needed to show that the new memories of sexual abuse tolled, or stopped the SOL from running and that the proverbial clock did not start until those memories of rape first surfaced.

I never met Jean Wehner (Jane Doe) before or during the lawsuit, and that was a good thing. We did not want anyone to think we corroborated our stories about what happened to us. Jean and I were kept apart throughout our entire case. I didn't have any idea who she was, and I only knew her as Jane Doe. I was aware that she graduated from Keough ahead of me in 1971. I did not testify at the hearing for the defense's Motion to Dismiss until Jean's testimony was completed. We entered and exited the courthouse through separate doors.

I was extremely nervous on the first day of my testimony. I knew what was involved in the legal proceeding, that I would be sworn in and questioned about my claim in open court. I knew there were people from the news stations present in the courtroom. I also knew that for their motion to be granted, the defense had to prove the three points they claimed in their Motion to Dismiss. My job was to respond honestly to the questions they would ask me.

Once again, the opposing lawyers took turns questioning me. I handled myself well through most of the inquiries. However, on one occasion, Harrison, the lawyer representing the nuns, called me by my maiden name, Harris, instead of Jane Roe. He said, "Well, Ms. Harris you claim that Father Maskell...." Thankfully, he was cut short by an objection from my lawyers who stated that we had been granted leave to use pseudonyms in our case to remain anonymous since the case involved sensitive sexual abuse. It was obvious to me that Harrison was attempting to upset me. I had made it known during my deposition with him that I did not want my identity made public. My maiden name, under which I was known at Keough, was Harris. Harrison knew I did not want to reveal that in open court.

I did not like Harrison at all, and I was not shy about that fact. As fate would have it, Mr. Harrison died from a rare lung infection during the Doe/Roe case. I would never wish such a thing on anyone, but I certainly shed no tears for him.

The opposing lawyers continued to question me for most of the day. They asked me to describe the douche bag. I knew I had enough time to elaborate, so I began my answer with, "Well the douche bag and the enema bag were one and the same apparatus. Maskell would change the tips on the end of the bag depending on what he was in the mood for that day." As I continued to explain further, the opposing lawyer objected to my detailed answer. The Judge reminded him that he couldn't object to his own question, so I continued to describe in detail how Maskell administered a douche to me. These questions were harsh but after answering questions in the written form in Interrogatories and in the oral form during six days of Depositions, I wanted the public to hear what I had to say.

The most effective argument the defense had against Jane Doe and me was that recovered memory was not admissible at trial because it is not generally accepted in the medical and or scientific community. This argument is called the Frye-Reed Standard.

As the Court stated in Reed v. State, 283 Md. 374 (1978), "general acceptance means just that; the answer cannot vary from case to case...it becomes the threshold question of admissibility, to be resolved as a matter of law before the court exercises its discretion in applying all criteria to a proffered expert."

Ultimately, Judge Caplin determined that the recovered memories I had experienced, did not stop the SOL from running. This meant that I had three years from the age of majority to file my lawsuit, which was age twenty-one. Losing Doe/Roe devastated me. I sank into depression as I wondered what my next steps would be.

CHAPTER 10

LIFE AFTER DOE/ROE

Looking back, I see how the Doe/Roe case consumed me. Regurgitating the details of what Maskell did to me, put me back into his office. However, reliving the abuse also made me stronger. I had a lot of fight left in me.

My lawyers took the Doe/Roe case before the Maryland Court of Appeals in Annapolis, but the decision by the lower court stood. My dad saw how losing the case was eating me up; when I approached him about filing a Writ of Certiorari to the Supreme Court, he didn't question me. The writ is an order by the supreme judicial court to an inferior tribunal (lower court) to certify and send its records in a particular case to the higher court to enable it to correct any errors or irregularities that may have taken place in the proceedings. The Supreme Court is the highest court in the federal judiciary of the United States and has ultimate appellate jurisdiction over all federal and state court cases. This High Court can hear any appellate case that presents a Constitutional question of federal law. When this Court decides to hear such a case it grants *certiorari* which simply means they will decide the case. Traditionally, it uses a narrow discretion to select which cases it will hear.

I didn't want to leave any stone unturned. I believed in justice and at the time I believed that by some miracle, the Supreme Court would hear me. My dad told me the case was over and that the high court would never hear the case because the SOL was well settled law. I was blind to this and would not take "no" for an answer.

I located an Appellant Attorney who agreed to file the writ even though it was more than a long shot. My dad funded the endeavor even though he knew it was hopeless, because he wanted to show me his unconditional support. Needless to say, my writ was turned down and I had to accept that the church had won. Maskell was free and he got away with all the evil things he did to me and God knows how many others. My dad's support meant the world to me and

CHAPTER 10

it brought us closer than I ever thought possible. Looking back, I believe filing the writ was part of my healing process. It ultimately freed me to get on with my life.

I wanted to be a lawyer. I knew I had a long road ahead of me since I only had a high school diploma, but I was not going to let that get in my way. I had taken a few courses at the Catonsville Community College (CCC, now known as The Community College of Baltimore County) over the last several years. I felt I had to start somewhere to achieve my goal of getting into law school.

I continued my studies at CCC and graduated from there with Honors and with my Associate Degree in General Studies. This didn't come easy to me, because it had been a long time since I studied subjects like algebra, history and science. I had to enroll in remedial math and English classes in order to maintain a decent GPA (Grade Point Average.) I hadn't learned anything during those last two years at Keough, other than survival skills. I had some backstepping to do if I was going to get my Bachelor's Degree.

My AA Degree from CCC enabled me to transfer into the University of Maryland Baltimore County (UMBC) and start there as a third-year college student. At UMBC I majored in Social Work and interned at the Public Defender's Office. There I could be more involved in law. I worked with juvenile offenders there and kept my focus on law. I achieved my Bachelor's degree in Social Work, which served as a stepping stone for me to get into law school.

SURVIVORS NETWORK OF THOSE ABUSED BY PRIESTS (SNAP)

I believed I had fully come to terms with being abused in high school and that I could manage anything, but I couldn't. I had difficulty concentrating and I became very depressed. My husband Randy encouraged me to finish my education and he took over a lot of the daily chores around the house to free up my time. That, along with staying involved with my children, kept me going. I wasn't one for going to a therapist, but I felt I could use some kind of help. I wanted to talk to someone who truly understood what I was going through.

I found a support group online comprised of survivors of clergy abuse and their supporters: The Survivors Network of those Abused by Priests (SNAP.) Wow! There was a group for survivors of priest abuse? I was not alone! I learned there are a lot of us out there and we can help each other through SNAP.

Initially SNAP focused on helping survivors of sexual abuse from the Roman Catholic Church, but it now has branches for survivors from other religious groups: SNAP Presbyterian, SNAP Orthodox and SNAP Baptist as well as for non-religious groups including the Boy Scouts and their families. Currently there are 12,000 members of SNAP with branches in fifty-six countries.

I joined SNAP and soon participated in their online chat groups. The people at SNAP helped me a great deal with my own healing. In turn, I learned how to help other survivors within SNAP. I wanted to learn as much as I could about how other survivors coped with the sadness and memories that often plague victims of childhood sexual abuse. I wanted to make a difference.

LAW SCHOOL

I desired a clear understanding of the law to fully understand exactly why the Doe/Roe case was dismissed before it got started.

I crawled out of my self-pity hole and decided to apply to law school to pursue my dream of becoming an attorney. During the depositions in the Doe/Roe case, I said that I wanted to be a lawyer and was subsequently mocked by the church lawyers. They laughed at me. This made me more determined to become an attorney--an attorney who would not thrive on other people's misery as those opposing me in the Doe/Roe case seemed to do.

Just getting into law school was an uphill climb. I first had to pass the Law School Admission Test (LSAT), a timed test designed to assess logical and verbal reasoning proficiency, as well as reading comprehension. These tests are designed to weed out people who have difficulty thinking fast, on their feet. I needed to score high enough to beat most of the other people taking the LSAT who were trying to get into one of the two accredited law schools in Maryland – University of

Baltimore School of Law, where my dad, brother, uncle and 2 cousins had gone and the University of Maryland School of Law, now known as University of Maryland Francis King Carey School of Law. I also had to have a high enough GPA, 3.25 for the University of Baltimore and 3.57 for the University of Maryland.

These tests were so difficult to pass that most, if not all, the law school applicants took an LSAT prep course before attempting to pass the exam. I took the prep course, which was a real eye-opener. The test is based on logic, reasoning, and critical thinking. One of my professors once described critical thinking as "thinking about thinking." Complex questions involving extensive problem solving, are presented and each query must be answered in about 2 minutes to complete the LSAT in the time allowed. I never saw anything like the questions I faced in this exam. (If you search 'LSAT Prep Courses' online you can see examples of test questions that will boggle your mind.)

As if the questions weren't challenging enough, about five minutes after I began my test, a young woman sitting about four seats behind me, ran out of the room crying hysterically. I did as I had been instructed to do in my prep course. If such a situation presented itself...I would focus on my test questions.

Every day, after taking the LSAT, I would look anxiously through the mail to see if my score was within the acceptance range. The acceptance rate at the University of Maryland Law School was 47.7%, with median LSAT score 158 and median GPA 3.56. The University of Baltimore acceptance rate was 57.42%, with median LSAT score 152 and median GPA 3.25. My LSAT score was high enough, so I submitted my score along with my undergrad transcripts and a cover letter to both of the Maryland Law Schools stating why I wanted to become an attorney. I was delighted to learn that I was accepted by both of the law schools' part time evening divisions. I elected to attend the University of Maryland School of Law because that school taught the theory behind the law. The University of Baltimore Law School seemed focused more on the "bare-bones" of law (just the facts.)

Law school was more than tough. At times I felt like I was drowning. I studied day and night. Some of the younger students asked me why I tried so hard. I told them that I was a lot older than they were and I wouldn't get a second chance to become an attorney. I joined four other older students to form a study group. We met every evening after class and reviewed everything that had been covered. Things went well for the most part.

A TASTE OF HELL

I often wondered if I had been a really evil person in a past life because I felt I had experienced more than a fair share of misery. Randy's Mom, Mary, suffered a heart attack during my first semester of law school. She seemed to be recovering well and elected to stay with a relative in Columbia, Maryland until she fully recovered. Mary loved her independence and decided, on her own, to cook an egg for breakfast. She was not familiar with gas stoves as she had an electric one at her home in Bowie, Maryland. Her relative's stove had gas burners. Somehow her robe caught fire while she was cooking the egg. Mary was taken to the Burn Center at Johns Hopkins. The attending nurses there recognized Randy from when his first wife was in the same burn unit fighting for her life after a fiery automobile accident, a battle she lost. Randy's Mom, Mary, passed away from her injuries about a week after being admitted.

Just a few weeks after we lost Randy's Mom in the horrible accident, our first grandchild, Ronnie, died suddenly just before his third birthday. He was a bright little boy, full of energy and a picture of health. An autopsy was performed to determine the cause of his death. The coroner determined that Ronnie had a very rare brain disorder which caused a fatal seizure.

Randy and I often wonder if Agent Orange (AO), to which he was exposed when he served in Vietnam, could have caused Ronnie's rare neurological disorder. AO was a powerful herbicide used by the US military to defoliate the jungles of Vietnam from 1961-1971. Over thirteen million gallons of AO were sprayed over the dense vegetation in Vietnam to remove concealment used by the Viet Cong. AO contained dioxin so extremely toxic that it was eventually banned.

Many Vietnam Vets who were subjected to the harmful chemicals in AO continue to suffer serious health issues resulting from their exposure. Studies have shown that the herbicide caused significant genetic damage to the DNA of Vets and support the possibility that genetic mutations could pass onto the children and grandchildren of those exposed. The Veteran Administration (VA) recognizes certain birth defects found in the children of these Vets as being caused by AO exposure. I will never know for sure, but I can't help thinking that AO caused little Ronnie's illness.

FATAL FALL

Things once again calmed down, but only for about a month before I found my dad in his home unconscious at the bottom of the stairs. I had been visiting my dad several times a week to take him dinner and talk about my law courses. He loved hearing how much I enjoyed the challenges of law school and reminisced about his own law school experiences.

On that occasion, my dad had fallen down a flight of steps sometime before I arrived. I called 911 and the paramedics transported him to the Shock Trauma Unit at the University of Maryland Hospital in Baltimore. He was treated there and it was determined that he suffered an Intracerebral hemorrhage ("ICH") which is when blood suddenly bursts into brain tissue, causing damage to the brain. My dad's brain bleed was so severe, it resulted in paralysis causing him to be unable to communicate. There was nothing that could be done for him other than palliative care. I took my dad to my home. Fortunately, I was able to hire nurse's aides to help care for him. The days started with tube feeding, bathing, range of motion exercises and other therapies. Dad passed away in my home six months after his fall.

I had become good at putting things on the back burner in my head, but I felt like I was having some sort of nervous breakdown. I went to the assistant dean of my law school to inquire about lessening my work load that semester. I asked the dean if it would be possible for me to move my contract law class to the following semester. She was very sympathetic about my losing three close family members, but explained how that wouldn't be fair to the other students if their work load were greater than mine. It might be seen as my having an unfair advantage. That, coupled with the fact that I would lose my place in the school if I took any time off, made me persevere. I knew my dad would want me to press on.

I told the dean I would be back after the weekend to continue my studies. I figured there would be time for grieving after I graduated. I completed my courses and earned my Juris Doctor Degree (JD) two and a half years later. I passed the Bar exam on my first try and was ready to conquer the world at last.

CHAPTER 11

LEGAL BATTLES

As an attorney, I maintain a solo law practice focused on helping people with issues involving disability, personal injury, child custody and basic general law. As an associate attorney at a Baltimore law firm focused on lead poison, I represented a young boy who suffered cognitive decline due to exposure to lead paint in his home. This was my first jury trial. I was awarded an $87,000 settlement for my client to help pay for his education. That case was featured in the local law newspaper, *The Daily Record*, February 19, 2008.

Currently, I help victims of childhood sexual abuse in their quest to seek justice. I have testified for many years in the Maryland Legislature for SOL reform. After the Doe/Roe case, the SOL for childhood sexual abuse cases was extended from age twenty-one to age twenty-five. In

2018, the SOL was extended to age thirty-eight. Why extend the time limit for victims of childhood sexual assault to sue the perpetrator? We now have a greater understanding of the reasons why persons harmed by childhood sexual abuse take so long to come forward. Studies have shown that the average age that a survivor of childhood sexual abuse comes forward to talk about it, is fifty-two.

Childhood sexual abuse is one of the most traumatic physical and psychological betrayals that one could experience. Many abusers use threats of violence to keep victims quiet. In my case I was threatened with a gun and told I'd be institutionalized. The injured parties often dissociate and block out the sexual trauma while it happens as a means of survival. These blocked or *repressed* memories often resurface later in life. The residual effects of childhood sexual abuse last a lifetime. I continue to fight for SOL reform with the hope of seeing it completely abolished. I believe victims should be allowed to file lawsuits, no matter how long ago the sexual abuse occurred.

REPRESSED MEMORY TODAY

We have learned a great deal about repressed memory since the 1990s. It is now generally accepted within the health and legal communities. In 2014, a Maryland Trial Court allowed testimony about repressed memory. *Dixson v. Beattie, Case No. 37501- Montgomery County Circuit Ct, MD, May 7, 2014.* The Plaintiff in this case presented an expert witness to testify that dissociative amnesia or repressed memory is routinely acknowledged in the scientific community. Moreover, it has been repeatedly observed clinically and recognized scientifically in peer-reviewed journal articles. *(Joyanna Lee Silberg, PhDs testimony in Dixson v. Beattie)* The defendant's expert witness countered with his testimony, "dissociative disorder or repressed memory is not accepted in the scientific community." *(Mr. Harrison Pope, M.D. testimony in Dixson v. Beattie)*

At the conclusion of this case, Judge Ronald B. Rubin issued a statement saying that "dissociative amnesia has been sufficiently tested by the psychiatric community using research methods and is generally accepted."

I would have won against the opposing lawyer's Motion to Dismiss in Doe/Roe had repressed memory been generally accepted in 1995. I would have had my day in court.

WHO KILLED SISTER CESNIK?

As I stated before, many of the caring members of SNAP have helped me with my healing over the years. In turn I have used my own coping methods along with my counseling skills to help other survivors of childhood sexual abuse move forward. In 2014, the Maryland Director of SNAP, Frank Dingle, called to tell me about a group of women on Facebook who were going after Maskell, determined to bring him down as an abuser and prove his involvement in the murder of Sister Catherine Cesnik, SSND. Frank and I had worked together over the previous decade advocating for SOL reform and helping other victims of sexual abuse. He knew my story well, which is why he thought I would be interested in checking out the group going after my abuser. My first reaction was that it sounded like the women were beating a dead horse considering Maskell. He, with the help of the AOB, had successfully evaded accountability in my Doe/ Roe case back in 1995 and he was deceased. Nevertheless, curiosity got the best of me and I looked into the group and the women who were investigating the murder of Sister Cathy, along with the rampant sexual abuse at Keough. They had started a Facebook page, "Justice for Catherine Cesnik and Joyce Malecki." Many unanswered questions remained about Maskell and the murder of Sister Cathy, as well as his unbridled sex ring which included Father Neil Magnus and police officers. I thought that social media might be just the right place to shed light on the unsolved case.

JOYCE AND CATHY

I believe that Sister Catherine Cesnik was brutally murdered for trying to help the students who confided in her about Maskell's sexually abusing them. Sister Cathy taught English and Drama at Keough and truly cared about her students. She was dedicated and would do anything she could to make sure her girls were safe. My friend, Gemma Hoskins, one of the founders of the Justice page, has made it her life's goal to find out what really happened to Sister Cathy. Gemma was featured in *The Keepers* as one of the top researchers digging into Cathy's murder and has stated that it was Sister Cathy who inspired her to become a teacher. Although I didn't know Sister Cathy well, I've learned from her past students that she was a sincere, caring, teacher; always there for her girls.

Sister Cathy went shopping at the iconic Edmondson Village Shopping Center on November 7, 1969 and never returned. It was determined that she cashed her $255 paycheck at the First National Bank in Catonsville on the way and purchased dinner rolls at Muhley's Bakery, which was located in the Hecht Company across from the shopping village. A witness, Juhiana Bertaldi, stated in *The Keepers* that Cathy was planning to shop for an engagement present for her sister that evening.

A hunter discovered Sister Cathy's dead body on January 3, 1970 near a garbage dump in a remote area of Lansdowne, Maryland. The autopsy was performed by Werner Uri Spitz, a renown forensic pathologist who has worked on several high-profile cases. Spitz determined that Sister Cathy died from intracerebral hemorrhage caused by blunt force trauma to her left temple. Mystery surrounds the reasons Sister was murdered. Police officials speculated that whoever dumped Sister Cathy's body, had to know the area well because the dump was difficult to find, especially in the dark when Sister Cathy went missing. This case remains unsolved.

The similarities between Sister Cathy's murder and that of Joyce Malecki are striking. Both women were members of St. Clement Church, where Father Maskell served as an assistant pastor. Joyce attended "retreats" there and would have spent time around Maskell. Moreover, Joyce allegedly told Maskell if he ever touched her little sister, she would kill him.

Joyce went Christmas shopping at Harundale Mall located in Glen Burnie on November 11, 1969. Her disappearance on this date occurred just four days after the disappearance of Sister Cathy. She lived less than a mile away from where Sister Cathy was found. Hunters discovered Joyce's body partially immersed in the water of the Little

Patuxent River at Fort Meade, on federal property, just a few miles from where Sister Cathy's body was found. Her hands were tied behind her back and she had wounds on her body indicating a struggle. Dr. Isidore Mihalakis performed the autopsy and determined that she had been bound and either strangled or drowned. He noted a deep wound on her throat that appeared to be made by a knife and approximately fifteen lacerations on her neck, but determined these injuries would not have caused her death. There were several FBI agents who believed there could have been a link between the two murders, but that was never proven. This case also remains unsolved.

I decided to join the "Justice for Catherine Cesnik and Joyce Malecki" Facebook page and post a message revealing that I was Jane Roe of the Doe/Roe case and willing to help the group unravel some of the questions surrounding Maskell, Sister Cathy and Joyce. I immediately received an outpouring of praise and support from the members of the group and was welcomed as a valued asset. I was very grateful to experience so many sincere well wishes on the

Justice for Sister Cathy page, which now has over 120,000 members.

Gemma Hoskins and Abbie Schaub, the two brave women who started this new grassroots investigation had graduated from Keough a year ahead of me, in 1971. The Facebook group grew as more survivors of Father Maskell came forward and additional facts about the rampant sexual abuse at Keough surfaced. We began to learn things about Sister Cathy's cold case that the police should have uncovered back in 1969, when the murder occurred.

In 2014, Gemma invited me to a meeting she organized at her home where some members of the group planned to get together in the hopes of uncovering more details about the case. Gemma is a serious investigator determined to gather as much information about this case as possible. She was the "Nancy Drew" of the group. Abbie is an excellent researcher who had dug up much of the history behind the case. With social media, we could bring this cold case to the public like never before.

Randy and I pulled up to Gemma's house where she warmly greeted us and introduced us to the people there. I met Tom Nugent, a former reporter for the *Baltimore Sun Paper* who had written an informative story about Sister Cathy's murder back in 2006. Tom always believed the case was more complex than anyone imagined and that there had been a massive cover-up. Tom had interviewed several retired detectives, who confirmed they had been pressured to back off from Maskell throughout their investigations in 1969 and the early 1970s. Tom was open and easygoing and I was impressed with the amount of detail he had uncovered while researching this case.

I also met a retired police detective at the meeting, who went by the name "Deep Throat." Deep Throat didn't want to reveal his identity because, even after all these years, he feared repercussions from higher-ups in the police force that had instructed him to back off investigating Maskell. He spoke about how many times he and his partner were closing in on Maskell, they were ordered to back off. Apparently, Maskell had many friends in high places who protected him.

Whether these friends were involved in the sexual abuse was yet to be discovered.

I also met *Huffington Post* journalist, Laura Bassett, at the meeting. Laura later asked me if she could interview me for a story about the case that she was working on. Laura was very friendly and seemed to be greatly moved when she heard about all the sex abuse that Maskell had gotten away with during his time at Keough. Additionally, the unsolved murders of Sister Cathy and Joyce Malecki definitely were the makings of a story that needed to be told. Laura's story "Buried in Baltimore: The Mysterious Murder of a Nun Who Knew Too Much" can be found online at: https://www.huffpost.com/entry/cesnik-nun-murder-maskell

Over the next several weeks I received phone calls and emails from several investigative reporters. I often called Tom Nugent to ask if he had heard of reporters who wanted to interview me about Maskell before I agreed to be questioned. Tom was more than helpful and we became good friends. My name was out there on social media and I was more than willing to share my story, although I remained a bit apprehensive.

On one occasion, I received a phone call from Ryan White and Jessica (Jess) Hargrove, telling me they were gathering information about the abuse that occurred at Keough, as well as about the murder of Sister Cathy for a documentary. Jess asked if I would be willing to talk to them about my part in the Doe/Roe case and the abuse I endured at Keough. I agreed to meet them at a local Panera Bread because I was apprehensive about having them come to my home since I didn't know them. I revealed to them much of what happened to me while we drank tea at Panera's. We talked for over an hour after which Ryan asked me if I would be willing to be interviewed on camera about everything I had just told them. I agreed and thus I was brought into the making of *The Keepers*.

CHAPTER 12

THE MAKING OF THE KEEPERS

Jessica Hargrave, producer, and Ryan White, director of Tripod Media, flew from their homes in California to Baltimore about once a month to interview and film the people affiliated with Maskell's sexual abuse ring at Keough and the murders of Sister Cathy Cesnik and Joyce Malecki. They always called to let me know what days were good for them to interview me so I could pick what would work best for me. Ryan usually questioned me for about four hours while Jess took notes and John Benam, photographer, followed us around with his camera. We enjoyed taking breaks when I would share several of my older photo albums and Keough memorabilia, some of which were used in the documentary.

The team got to know Randy and my daughter Annette, who were always with me during the filming. The film team also got to meet Alejandro, my Munchkin cat, and

Peanut, my daughter Christy's hedgehog. I like to bake, so I made fresh fruit pies, sweet bread, or cinnamon buns for interview days. It was a great way to lighten the mood and bring about a more relaxed atmosphere after talking about such troublesome times. We became good friends during the making of the documentary leading up to the release of *The Keepers* on May 19, 2017.

On one occasion, Gemma, Jess, Ryan, and I planned to take a field trip to Keough. I had not been back to Keough since graduating in 1972 and this was a big step for me to take. As we pulled up to the front of the building, I had an awful feeling in the pit of my stomach. Even so, I wanted to get a closer look at the white concrete grid outside of the remote fire door leading to Maskell's old office. I remembered how Maskell would let me stand behind the grid to get fresh air and smoke during some of my sessions with him. Gemma and I started looking around that door when a short middle-aged woman came out from the building and asked if she could help us.

Gemma identified us as Keough alums who were very much interested in touring the school building. The woman introduced herself and told us to follow her through the main entrance into the general office where we could ask if there was anyone available who could show us around. In an attempt to get someone to show us around, Gemma told a younger woman in the office that we were proud to be Keough alumnae, and our friends Jess and Ryan were thinking about sending their daughter to the Holy Angel Catholic Elementary School now operating at Keough along with the high school. Delighted to see we were interested in the school, this woman smiled as she got up and offered to give us a general tour of the building.

I kept whispering to Gemma that I felt like I was going to throw up as we walked down the hall leading to where Maskell's office used to be. When we reached the chapel, we asked if we could go inside. Jess kept our tour guide occupied looking at lockers and stuff in the hallway while Gemma, Ryan and I went into the chapel. Once inside, I showed them where the door leading into Maskell's office was and talked about how he took me into the chapel directly from his office. I told them he kept the main door to the chapel locked and used the altar as a gynecological examining table. Ryan used his phone to film me describing the atrocities that occurred in the chapel. I started to feel dizzy and told Gemma I felt like I was going to throw up again. It was chilling!

The high school portion of Keough remained open until the end of the 2015-16 school year. There were teenage girls attending classes when we were touring the school. As we walked back down the hall toward the main office, I noticed the steps leading up to the second floor. Several high school girls ran happily down the steps and passed us, laughing, on their way to their next class. When I saw how young these girls were, I felt an overwhelming sadness. I couldn't help thinking how young I was back when I attended high school there. A kid! I was just a kid like the girls that ran by us. How could a man, a priest, do the things he did to me when I was so young? He should have been protecting us from harm, not inflicting it.

On another occasion Jess and Ryan told me they had been meeting with Jean (Jane Doe) and speaking with her about her dealings with Maskell. I told them that I always admired Jean and was thankful she had come forward to expose Maskell back in the 90's but I had never met her during the Doe/Roe case or even in all the years since. This seemed to surprise Jess and Ryan. I explained how the lawyers did not want us to meet each other during the case because people could claim we collaborated on our memories of the abuse. At the time, both of us were in different places in our healing. Jess asked how I would feel about meeting Jean for our documentary. I thought it would be wonderful to finally meet her and we scheduled a field day to travel to Jean's home.

It is difficult to explain the rush of emotions I experienced when Jean welcomed me into her home. Our eyes met and we embraced each other. All the pain we had been through during the Doe/Roe case ran through my mind. I was more than delighted to finally meet Jean and sit down to talk with her after all those years. John followed us around with his camera to capture the meeting. It was golden. Since that day Jean and I have become good buddies and I treasure her friendship.

PIE DAY

Everyone knew I enjoyed baking because I found it calming and cheaper than talking to a therapist about my abuse. To lighten the mood, Ryan and Jess suggested we spend a day talking about and filming me baking. I thought this was a great idea and was delighted when my daughter, Annette, offered to help me. To prepare for "pie day" I set out the ingredients I would be using ahead of time, like they do on TV cooking shows. Soon after the team arrived, Annette and I had all kinds of things cooking. I was rolling out pie dough while Annette squeezed fresh lemons for the lemon meringue pie. John expertly maneuvered around us with his camera equipment, capturing some prime moments on video. It was a bit hectic and at one point, Annette wondered why her lemon pie filling wasn't thickening until she noticed the burner was not turned on. It was a great day and a much-needed break from the dark topics covered in the docuseries.

On another occasion, in March 2016, the documentary team followed me around in downtown Annapolis when I testified before the House Judiciary Committee for SOL reform. There, I had the opportunity to explain how victims of childhood sexual abuse needed time to come to terms with the horrors they endured which meant that they typically didn't come forward to report their abuse until later in life; the average age being fifty-two. That is why extending the SOL is especially important for survivors to acquire justice.

Conversely, the church lawyer, Kevin Murphy, testified that the SOL was intended to encourage victims to report abuse earlier which would enable the church to stop named abusers from harming someone else. He added that the church did not want the abusers to go unpunished or to abuse others. This coming from an organization that enabled countless priests to abuse children in every way imaginable greatly angered me. However, watching their lies captured on camera was promising to me because the records show how the church has enabled predator priests to continue abusing children for hundreds of years. The public could see how the individuals representing the Catholic "corporation" used the same phony excuses to influence the Judiciary Committee to maintain the archaic SOL to prevent victims from realizing justice.

A TEST OF STRENGTH

I looked forward to the production of our documentary and was more than happy to take the time needed to achieve this. However, in December 2015, my annual mammogram showed a suspicious area in my right breast which required further investigation. As I mentioned in Chapter 8, I had a substantial family history of breast cancer, plus I carried the BRCA I mutation gene, which put me at an extremely high risk of developing breast cancer. After weighing all my options, I underwent a double mastectomy in January 2016. I knew this wasn't going to be an easy operation since I wanted to undergo immediate reconstruction after the removal of my breasts. The emotional toll hit me hard as I remembered how awful I felt watching my mom face her single mastectomy years ago. Frankly, I was terrified.

I scheduled a meeting with my primary surgeon and the two reconstruction surgeons at the Breast Reconstruction and Restoration Center at Mercy Hospital in Baltimore City. I was very fortunate to be a patient at Mercy, which is considered one of the best centers for state-of-the-art breast reconstruction and restoration techniques following breast cancer surgery. Immediately after my mastectomy, two expert surgeons, Dr. Bernie Butler and Dr. Brendan Myers would perform a Superior Gluteal Artery Perforator flap breast reconstruction (SGAP) on me. The SGAP procedure is a microsurgical breast reconstruction treatment option for patients following a double mastectomy. Basically, it involves using buttock tissue for reconstruction of both breasts during the same surgery. Trying to remain optimistic, I looked at it as a win, win situation since following my surgery I would have a smaller butt and bigger boobs. Joking aside, the surgeons informed me that the ordeal would take about sixteen hours to complete, which was very scary.

My recovery was difficult and I struggled just to sit up in bed after waking up from the long ordeal. The nurses informed me they performed range of motion exercises on my arms and legs throughout my procedure to keep my muscles active. Even so, I couldn't even stand up without the assistance of two people. Walking was a real challenge and initially I found myself dragging my feet like Frankenstein, partly because of the muscle that was removed from my buttocks. I remained in the hospital for the week of the January 2016 Baltimore Blizzard. Over two feet of snow fell between January 22 to January 23, breaking records for a single day snowfall. When I was finally released from the hospital, I had five separate drains in place which required frequent attention. With Randy's help and that of my three daughters Lisa, Christy and Annette, I slowly recovered and was soon up and about on my own.

Following the surgery, my surgeon called to inform me that my biopsy revealed that I had *ductal carcinoma in situ* in my left breast. Fortunately, since the cancer was discovered early, I did not require chemotherapy or radiation treatments. I shared my ordeal with Jess, Ryan and John and spoke on camera about how I managed to get through this very emotional, life changing illness. I recalled how I approached the cancer as though it was happening to someone else and I was merely watching. This was oddly reminiscent of how I dealt with Maskell's abuse.

AN ADVENTURE IN PENNSYLVANIA

After I recovered from my surgery, the documentary crew and I decided to take another field trip. This time we planned to travel to Pennsylvania to visit my survivor friend, Donna. I first met Donna through the online justice group, and she shared her chilling story of how Maskell and his friends abused her back at Keough.

Donna greeted us at her front door and invited us inside where we gathered around her kitchen table. It was covered with a red and white gingham table cloth, creating a true country ambiance. On one side of her kitchen, Donna had filled shelves sitting in front of her spacious window with brightly colored translucent "Depression" glassware. I learned that this glassware gets its name from being produced between 1929-1939, during the Great Depression that began in the United States. The colorful patterns on the glasses and vases of pink, yellow, crystal, green and blue captured the sunlight and produced a rainbow effect in Donna's kitchen. The warm atmosphere was perfect and we spent the next several hours talking about our days at Keough when we were helpless under Maskell's control.

Donna told me she had followed my Doe/Roe case back in the 90s. She said she greatly admired me for coming forward at a time when most people couldn't believe that priests were capable of such abuse. Donna read the following beautiful poem she had written for me while John filmed us.

The Message

Honor and thanks be to She,

Who drugged down this road.

I looked dimly, and could see,

STAY; became my ode.

Down a low valley I slid,

The bottom was near.

Flickers of light, grasped I did,

Pulling me through fear.

Kings and giants She outlast!

Raising kids so kind.

CHAPTER 12

Only to be an outcast,

Helping ones behind.

I hold my head, not alone,

Proud, with you we meet.

Today you enter my home,

Now paths are complete.

Love, Donna

2016

To lighten the mood, Donna suggested we check out a warehouse nearby that sold all kinds of baking supplies. Everybody thought it would be a great idea for us to go out for lunch and stop by the warehouse on the way back to Donna's house. After we ate, John carried his camera equipment and started filming us as we entered the storage facility. We walked ahead of John and delighted in the vast rows of shelving that were full of everything imaginable needed for baking. I was like a kid in a candy store and filled our shopping cart with glass bowls, pie pans, measuring cups shaped like ducks and oven mitts decorated with chickens. It was nice to laugh given the seriousness of our documentary.

RANDY EXPRESSES HIS THOUGHTS OF LIVING WITH A SURVIVOR

Ryan and Jess thought it would be a good idea to interview Randy to learn what it was like for him being married to a survivor. So far Randy remained off camera with his main goal being to support me. The truth is, the residual effects of childhood sexual abuse touch everyone involved with the victim. There are times when I shut down and am difficult to read. I believe this is a residual side effect of how I survived through those years of abuse followed by years of confusion. Confusion about where I was in life and where I was going, as a mom, a student and a survivor, often filled my head. Randy was more than happy to share how he knew when I was in another place, consumed with thoughts of Maskell. When I relive the events at Keough on camera, it brought him into Maskell's office with me. In *The Keepers*, Randy shared how he felt when I told him I was going to law school after the loss of the Doe/Roe lawsuit and how watching me move forward after that loss made him feel. I actually learned from listening to Randy describe how he tried to help support me and my children through those days of determination. I felt more than ever that I was fortunate to have him in my life.

REACTIONS TO THE KEEPERS

Jess, Ryan, and John remained personable throughout the many weeks it took to complete the documentary. The carefully thought-out questions Ryan asked really brought the story to life. The many hours of interviewing touched on every aspect of my story. I was totally exhausted after each session and always needed several days to recuperate. It was impossible for me to describe what happened in Maskell's office without reliving it, but telling my story was incredibly important to me. This was definitely quality work by people who genuinely cared about the survivors and sought to bring justice to the victims.

When the documentary was nearly complete, Jess and Ryan visited my home to inform me that the story was going to be called *The Keepers*. What an amazing title! I loved it! I could immediately identify with the title since I had been a keeper of many dark secrets for so long. This was fantastic! When they told me that Netflix was going to air the documentary, I was ecstatic. I knew how many people Netflix reached, and this was bigger than I ever expected it to be. I thought back to when I was sixteen, afraid and naked in Maskell's office all those years ago. I never in my wildest dreams thought I would be able to talk about being raped, and now Netflix was going to broadcast my story all over the world. No words.

During the days leading up to the release of *The Keepers*, I was both excited and nervous. I could not help thinking about everything I had revealed about my abuse and I worried how the documentary would be received. Would people believe me? My mind raced back to Doe/Roe and how the church lawyers said I was a lying mental case. I told Randy I just wanted to come across as relatively normal in the documentary. I did not want people to think I was crazy. I was in an anxious state of mind.

I watched the preview of *The Keepers* several weeks before its release on May 19, 2017. I thought the preview was extremely well done and raised interest in the entire story of Keough, as well as the murders of Sister Cathy and Joyce Malecki. I remained anxious to see the documentary, but felt less worried about it at that point.

On the day the documentary aired, I experienced mixed feelings of joy and fear. I sat down with Randy and started to watch the first episode and experienced stomach pain to such a degree I had to see my doctor before I could continue watching the production. Armed with bismuth subsalicylate to calm my stomach, I turned on my TV once again. When I first saw myself on my flat screen, I was numb. I had not foreseen this reaction during the filming. The images on the screen seemed larger than life and there I was talking about my sexual abuse at the hands of Father Maskell. It was surreal for me. I used deep breathing exercises to calm myself and finally settled in to binge watch the entire series - at times through my tears.

To my delight, *The Keepers* received widespread positive reviews. People were enticed and many binged watched all seven episodes. The story included testimony from many people and involved a lot of facts. Ryan, Jess and their team were tasked with pulling out the most relevant information from over 800 hours of video to tell the story in seven, one hour-long episodes.

People heard our story, and they were moved by it. After *The Keepers* aired, when I went shopping at my local grocery store, I noticed people staring at me. They recognized me from the series! On one occasion, I saw a lady smiling at me and she came over and thanked me, asking if she could hug me. People came up to me to tell me they watched the documentary and they were very sorry for what I had gone through. Others came over to me and said they too were abused and they were ready to talk about it now. A guy at the gas station across from my local grocery store came over to me as I pumped my gas to tell me he thought I was amazing. I still receive many well wishes on Netflix's Facebook page dedicated to *The Keepers* which now has over 120,000 members. I also receive dozens of private messages of support from all over the world. I am humbled by the supportive recognition I experience. What a difference from Doe/Roe! I couldn't help thinking how the church knew all of this was true back when they called me a confused liar during the 1995 Doe/Roe case. Now they had to weather the storm *The Keepers* brought.

The numerous favorable responses from people around the world who watched *The Keepers,* reinforce my desire to advocate and continue to be an activist for victims of childhood sexual abuse. Every day more victims are finding their voice and coming forward to report their abuse, be it from the clergy, their coaches, or a family member. We shined a light on a dark situation, and it was wonderful. Survivors now know they are NOT alone!

A MESSAGE FROM A FAN

"Hi Teresa, I just started watching *The Keepers* and of course, as someone who has been a Catholic all my life, it has affected & troubled me deeply. You, in particular, have moved me so immensely. I'm only on episode 4 but I'm so amazed by how you went back to school and became a lawyer while still being an amazing mom to four children. Your husband's words resonated with me as an overwhelmed mom of only two young children! I broke eight vertebrae in my back shortly after giving birth to my first baby and in a nutshell, after always having been very career focused, things took quite a turn for me, but you've really inspired me. Thank you so much for sharing your story...you are an amazing woman and a true inspiration!!"

CHAPTER 13

PASTORAL GESTURES

THE APOLOGY LETTER

The Archdiocese of Baltimore (AOB) went from portraying me as an unstable, confused, money-hungry mental case during the 1995 Doe/Roe lawsuit to sending me a letter of apology in 2010, forty years after Maskell abused me. This letter read in part, "Please accept my apology on behalf of Archbishop (Edwin) O'Brien and the AOB for the suffering that has resulted from your experiences," signed by Alison D'Alessandro, director of the church's Office of Child and Youth Protection. The Archdiocese also offered me an opportunity to meet Archbishop O'Brien so he could offer me his personal regrets. I was through talking with their people dressed in outlandish outfits complete with fancy satin trim and eccentric hats. I do not trust men hiding behind golden crucifixes and other peculiar accessories. I declined the offer.

All I ever wanted from the AOB was a sincere apology for the sexual abuse I endured as a teenager and the release of Maskell's records. Their half-hearted apology was vague - "for suffering that has resulted from your experiences." I want them to say the words... "We are sorry we enabled Father Maskell to repeatedly use your naked body for self-pleasure when you were a teenager." This has yet to happen. I also want to see the records they have on Maskell from his psychological evaluations to the church order banning him from saying Mass.

MEDIATION

A mediation is an interactive process of resolving disputes without involving the judicial system. An impartial third party uses negotiation skills to assist the participants to reach a mutually acceptable agreement. The process is voluntary and informal, usually held in a conference room setting.

As more victims came forward to report being abused by their parish priests, the AOB began to offer them mediations as a "pastoral gesture." This reconciliation was a great way for the church to bolster their failing public relations.

The victim participating in such a mediation presents an "Impact Statement" to the church representative detailing how their sexual abuse negatively affected their life. The victim may also offer testimony about what the priest did to them. Subsequently, the church offers them monetary compensation and psychological counseling as a show of "good faith."

In 2011 my esteemed colleague, Attorney Joanne Suder, offered to arrange a mediation between myself and the AOB. Joanne is a leading authority on pedophile and sexual abuse cases who advocates for the rights of victims abused by people entrusted with their well-being. I had no other legal remedy for my case since the SOL had long passed, so I agreed to participate in a mediation.

The AOB's attorney initiated the negotiations by expressing regret for what happened to me at Keough without taking any responsibility for it. He first offered me $15,000 as a "pastoral gesture" and indicated that in no way should the offer be construed as an admission of guilt. "Of course not," I thought to myself. I responded by describing how Maskell performed "gynecological examinations" on me several times a week when I was a student at Keough. I spoke about the enema/douche bag and how it was used. It seemed like the church representatives felt a need to hear me elaborate on the particulars of my abuse before they would consider presenting a better offer.

In August 2018 in Harrisburg, Pennsylvania Attorney General Josh Shapiro disclosed the comprehensive findings of a two-year statewide investigation by the grand jury there. The abuse of children, a systematic cover-up over decades by officials of the church both in Pennsylvania and the Vatican was revealed. Additionally, the grand jury recommended that the criminal and civil statutes of limitations (SOL) be reformed in Pennsylvania.

Upon reading this extensive grand jury report, I learned that the church has guidelines that actually attach a price to each sexual act a clergy abuse victim endures. A chart that the Pennsylvania Attorney General uncovered in the church's secret archives during their 2018 grandy jury investigation there, shows guidelines the Diocese follow when they calculate a compensation amount for a victim of childhood sexual assault. I included this information below, because it may explain why it was necessary for me to vividly describe the sexual acts I endured to the church representatives during my mediation.

119

judgments of the Diocese in the payment of claims and in the purchase of silence. The chart appears as follows:

LEVEL OF ABUSE		RANGE OF PAYMENT
I.	Above clothing, genital fondling	$10,000 - $25,000
II.	Fondling under clothes; masturbation	$15,000 - $40,000
III.	Oral sex	$25,000 - $75,000
IV.	Sodomy; Intercourse	$50,000 - $175,000

The chart is footnoted with "Factors to consider for valuation within a range." Those "factors" are: number of occurrences; duration of abuse over time; age of victim; use of alcohol or drugs; apparent effect of abuse on victims (psychosis); and other aggravating circumstances.

To see the Pennsylvania compensation schedule online check out the following link: https://www.ncronline.org/news/accountability/grand-jury-report-reveals-decades-clergy-sex-abuse-altoona-johnstown-diocese.

According to the Pennsylvania compensation schedule an act of forced anal rape merits $50,000 - $175,000. How does one determine this? Should days of pain and bleeding after forced anal sex increase the compensation? Based on the guidelines, above clothing fondling merits $10,000 - $25,000. Does this mean each act of fondling merits $10,000? Father Maskell fondled my bare breasts dozens of times. Does that merit the full $25,000 compensation? Also, does rough fondling merit a higher compensation than a gentler fondling? I am disgusted with this chart and how the church goes about calculating compensation for childhood sexual abuse victims.

I went back and forth with the AOB throughout my mediation, being as explicit as possible about my various abuse sessions with Father Maskell. I revealed how Maskell chased me around his office when I was completely naked (except for my socks), tackled me, and inserted a suppository into my vagina. I talked about how Maskell made me sit on the toilet while he watched and how he insisted on teaching me the proper way to wipe myself. I divulged how I continue to experience strange phobias about using public toilets and how I excessively clean my toilet at home. I wanted the AOB to know that Maskell's perversions affected my life forever.

I relived my abuse as I described some of the things Maskell did to me. The entire two-day mediation process was very painful for me. I settled for $40,000 of which $11,732 paid for my legal fees. I considered the $28,268 I ultimately received akin to blood money and divided it among my children to help them pay for my grandchildren's braces and other needs.

I wanted the church to release the records they kept on Maskell and admit that there was a massive cover up which enabled him to abuse not only me but also many of my Keough sisters. I wanted them to admit how they were aware Maskell was a predator and merely transferred him from parish to parish as victims reported abuse.

I later learned from an anonymous source that it was the AOB consensus that since they were forced to spend a great deal of money on legal fees defending the church during the Doe/Rose case back in 1995, they didn't feel they should offer me more than a nominal amount at my mediation. In other words, they believed they had already spent too much money on me. This infuriated me because I couldn't understand why I should be slighted because they elected to spend thousands of dollars to quash the lawsuit against Maskell, which they knew to be credible.

As of May 2016, the AOB paid more than $472,000 in settlements to approximately sixteen victims of Father Maskell. *The Keepers* aired on May 17, 2017 after which more victims found the courage to come forward to report the sexual abuse, they suffered at Keough. The AOB was not legally obligated to compensate these victims in any way since the time for them to sue for damages (SOL) had long since passed, but it sought to maintain a positive stance by offering them a "pastoral gesture."

As numerous victims continue to step up to report their abuse, the AOB looks for ways to maintain damage control. Sunday sermons express great sorrow on behalf of the church for the abuse, while downplaying the number of predator priests. They claim the church is doing everything in their power to prevent priest abuse from happening again and offer their thoughts and prayers for those who suffered clergy abuse. These shows of sorrow and repentance are just words used to save face ... empty promises.

I believe the church should admit what Maskell did to me and allow me to see the records kept on him. I want them to admit to the massive cover up that enabled Maskell to abuse over one hundred individuals. I want them to admit how they were aware that Maskell was a predator back when he attended St. Mary's Seminary and yet allowed him to become a priest. The AOB must be held accountable for transferring him from parish to parish after his abuse was reported to them. Transferring Maskell enabled him to continue to harm children.

I believe the only reason the AOB acknowledges that their priests sexually abused children now, is because they got caught on a grand scale. Numerous brave victims have found their voice and stepped up to report their abuse. Thousands of priests have been credibly accused, which forced the church to respond. The AOB is in damage control mode.

THE FUTURE

We have a lot of work to do. The Pennsylvania Grand Jury report released on August 14, 2018 named more than three hundred priests creditably accused of child sexual abuse. I believe this report brought the huge extent of the suffering and injustice that victims face to the forefront. Many states are falling into place and calling on their Attorney Generals to investigate these crimes against children as they should have been investigated decades ago.

Currently, in Maryland, the Attorney General is actively interviewing victims and looking into records of the Baltimore Archdiocese, as an ongoing investigation into childhood sexual abuse. Their office is probing numerous confidential files kept by the church. I appeal to victims of sexual abuse in the state of Maryland: no matter how long ago, please report the abuse to The Maryland Attorney General office's investigator, Richard Wolf at rwolf@oag. state.md.us or call 410-576-6300. I reported my personal abuse to Mr. Wolf in an effort to shed more light on the rampant sex ring at Keough from 1969-1972. As of this writing, this investigation continues and the people involved in uncovering evidence are very much interested in hearing from anyone who may have any information about sexual abuse that occurred during this time.

The church claims to be taking action to stop the widespread abuse of children. Why now? I believe it's because they got caught. They had to do something. Thanks to the brave survivors who have come forth and shared their stories, victims are at least validated now. We have come a long way since the 1995 Doe/Roe case, but the legal drama and battle between the experts continues regarding the validity of repressed memory. We must keep the stories about the unbridled childhood sexual abuse in the media.

My friend, Abbie Schaub, the diligent researcher featured in *The Keepers*, has been working along with me and many other concerned advocates to change the SOL to better serve victims of childhood sexual abuse. She once said, "It would be a permanent, positive legacy from *The Keepers* story if we can change those laws to reveal other hidden predators." If our story helps prevent just one child from falling prey to a predator priest, I will consider it a great success. And in the event children continue to suffer sexual abuse, be it from priests, teachers, coaches or anyone holding a position of power, it is my sincere hope that when these victims are strong enough to come forward to report their abuse, they will not have to battle the archaic SOL law to realize justice.

BUT IT'S JUST A FEW PRIESTS, RIGHT?

People often ask me why I continue to talk about and expose predator priests given the fact that my sexual abuse by the clergy happened so long ago. Many agree the church has failed to stop predator priests from sexually abusing vulnerable children for centuries. Yet I often hear, "Those things don't happen anymore. Things have changed…right??" The church tries to convince its followers that the systemic abuse by its clergy, enabled by the church hierarchy, has stopped. It has not. Numerous faithful followers insist it was only a few priests who abused. This is also false. Childhood sexual abuse involves thousands of priests all over the world. See: The Bishop Accountability website which documents the ongoing crisis of priest sexual abuse. http://www.bishop-accountability.org/ Yes, my abuse occurred long ago but young people all over the world continue to suffer sexual abuse. We must make it stop.

Another resource which documents the continuing abuse by the clergy as well as by laypeople is SNAP, an organization which I spoke about earlier in my book. This is one of the oldest support groups for victims of clergy abuse. See: https://www.snapnetwork.org/. SNAP continues to help victims and reports current sexual abuse situations be it from the clergy or others.

There is a lot of information about Father Maskell on the internet. To read more about his life just conduct an online search of his name.

CHAPTER 14

COLLATERAL DAMAGE

UNEXPRESSED EMOTIONS WILL NEVER
DIE. THEY ARE BURIED ALIVE AND WILL
COME FORTH LATER IN UGLIER WAYS...
SIGMUND FREUD

FORGOTTEN VICTIMS:
PARENTS

I really struggled to maintain a "normal" appearance both during and after my sessions with Maskell. Numerous people have asked me why I didn't tell my parents. Well, first of all, I had gone to Maskell for help to mend the broken communication between my parents and me. Things were not good between us. It was complicated. At that time, we never ever spoke of sex. It was a taboo topic and simply not something I could ever talk about with my parents. During my depositions in the Doe/Roe case, one of the most aggressive opposing lawyers (Mr. Harrison who represented the nuns) kept asking me why I didn't talk to my mom about the gynecological visits. Why didn't I tell her how Maskell was in the exam room with the doctor? He asked me how I learned about sex, demanding to know who explained sexual stuff to me. I told him the only vaguely sexual thing I had ever talked about with my mom was the movie for eighth-grade girls that explained menstruation. The movie was shown to the female students in the school hall at my grammar school, St. Williams. After the movie a doctor (the father of one of the students) spoke to us and answered a few general questions about our menstrual period. That was it as far as my Catholic education about sex. It was a topic that was off limits in my world at that time.

Nevertheless, the lawyer pressed for a longer answer and asked me if I thought Maskell fondling my breasts was sex. He asked what I regarded as sex. I replied that intercourse was sex. He then asked if I thought being naked on the priest's lap while he fondled my breasts was sex? I answered that when he put it that way, I supposed it was sex. I wasn't sure just how he wanted me to answer his demeaning questions. When he asked where I learned about the sex act, I told him from talking to my friends. He made fun of that off the record commenting that it must have been an interesting conversation with my friends when we spoke of sex. I agreed, it must have been a real eye opener.

I told the lawyer that the mere thought of telling my parents how Maskell made me take off all of my clothes was just too bizarre. Also, I totally believed what Maskell had embedded into my mind, that no one, not even my parents, would believe me over a priest. Additionally, there was the fact that he convinced me I was nothing, that I was expendable, that no one would miss me if he shot me and dumped my body somewhere.

My parents were trapped in this dreadful situation much as I was. They believed the words of the good priest. They were Catholic. They believed the priest was our savior and there to make things right. As a mother, I know they suffered watching me struggle in "teenage wasteland." Much like survivors, parents are victims too. Their mental torment during this time was collateral damage. The damage spilled over into my adulthood when I never spoke of Keough or my high school years with my parents.

SIBLINGS

I had grown apart from my three older brothers when I reached my teenage years. I found I had nothing in common with any of them, nothing to share about my days at Keough. My brothers were all destined to become highly educated professionals. Their conversations involved sophisticated knowledge that I lacked. Also, they, like many people back then, believed that girls were destined to get married and become stay-at-home mothers. I fell into that domestic role despite the fact that I possessed a brain yearning for knowledge.

I often wondered how things got so crazy. I missed the playful times I had spent as a child growing up with my brothers. The hot summer days we enjoyed together at the local Hunting Hills Swimming Pool seemed like a lifetime ago. I yearned for the long summer evenings I spent with my brother Mark, catching lightning bugs and staring at the stars far above us while sitting on my balcony. I missed watching the Catonsville fireworks together, playing board games like Risk, Stratego, and Monopoly. The excitement of Christmas morning and chocolate bunny candy on Easter .... all just distant memories.

Things changed. What could I share with my brothers? I certainly couldn't say, "Hey, today was weird. Father Maskell took all of my clothes off again."

To make matters worse, my brothers knew about the "searching of my purse," incident which made me out to be a hopeless druggie determined to throw my life away. I became withdrawn from my siblings and decided I had to fight this war I found myself trapped in, on my own. The loss of my relationship with my brothers, much like the loss of my relationship with my parents, was collateral damage.

FRIENDS

Dark secrets resided deep in my brain. My friends were concerned with their grades and their futures. Most of my friends were college bound and pursuing nursing or teaching careers. I was not. I found myself merely surviving day to day instead of planning for a career. My life was not my own. I was wrapped up in an unbelievable situation and needed to figure out how to pull myself together. I just wanted to appear normal.

Although I had shared my knowledge that Maskell was a pervert with most of my friends, I had to be careful for fear of him carrying out his threats of sending me to Montrose or shooting me. The days of hanging out and listening to music with my buddies were over. I was forced to grow up fast. I became isolated from just about everyone. Maybe my closest friends cared, I didn't know for sure, but losing old friendships was again collateral damage.

As time went on, however, I found a group of people very much like me. I discovered there were a lot of lost souls struggling to heal from being sexually abused. People I could talk to. People that truly understood. Joining SNAP and talking to other survivors brought me out of isolation and made me strong. I found that the more I helped other survivors, the more I helped myself. Eventually I found the courage to finish my education and realize my dream of becoming an attorney. Over the years I have formed meaningful relationships with people who truly understand me and share my beliefs. I make it my mission to try to help other survivors and fight alongside them for justice. Sharing my story has been difficult, but these acts of abuse had to be exposed if we are going to save future generations from harm. My newfound friendships help lessen the impact of losing old friends, collateral damage caused by my abuse.

CHILDREN OF SURVIVORS

There hasn't been enough said, what the children of parents who have been sexually abused, endure. The childhood sexual abuse of parents does not stop with them. Children are intuitive and they know when something is not right with mom or dad. They often grow up watching their survivor parent go through things they cannot understand. How can the children of the abused understand things that their abused parent doesn't even understand?

Intrusive memories of things that happened to me at Keough followed me whenever I had to submit to a gynecological examination. These memories or thoughts stick in my mind. Sometimes invading thoughts occur frequently and are very disturbing. After suffering abuse with Maskell and his doctor friend, I developed a great mistrust of doctors in general. I never wanted to go to the same doctor more than once, except when they followed me throughout one of my four pregnancies. Even then, soon after the delivery of my child, I sought out a new gynecologist. As time went on and my daughters got older, they often asked me why I kept changing doctors. I didn't know, other than I had tremendous trust issues stemming back to the betrayal of Father Maskell. The roller coaster ride of emotions has followed me throughout my entire life. There isn't one day that I don't hear, see or think about Maskell's abuse. Not one day!

My children had to deal with how I coped with being sexually abused. Sometimes I would stare out a window for hours and other times I would take long walks barely speaking. I suffered from PTSD, anxiety, mistrust and depression. When my children were old enough, I told them I was abused by a priest. Talking about what happened brought them a clearer understanding why I did some of the things I did. I fought hard to be present with my children, and as they grew older. It became important to me to let them know why I might seem a little different. This openness has brought me closer to my children than I ever felt possible and that is a good thing.

When I asked my oldest daughter, Lisa, if she had anything to add to my story, she said the following, "The horrifying glimpse I was given of the biggest pervert organization in recorded history will haunt me forever...My mother has always born the look of human suffering and now I know who to credit with that."

SELF PRESERVATION

Over the years I have developed many ways to cope with the residual problems I face from being abused. It has been difficult writing about some of my abuse in this book.

I have experienced stomach and sleep problems brought on by images where I relive my abuse. On occasion I have experienced personal "snap shots" out of nowhere of a "flash" of abuse. For example, a slap - seen and felt for a second - while I'm in the middle of a conversation, taking a walk, or doing household chores.

I often wonder how anyone other than a victim could truly understand another victim's thought process. The lucky among us have the ability to differentiate between the "now" and "then." To do so promotes healing and personal growth. Less fortunate victims find themselves trapped in the "then" and the "snap shots" are not a snap, but a perpetual visual hell that causes physical pain and mental torment.

"Triggers" is an important word in a survivor's world. It is used to describe how a sound, smell, object, or feeling can bring back buried tormenting memories. Survivors need lots of reinforcement, support and reassurance to realize they are not alone or insane. I often respond to survivors who write to me. I assure and reassure them that they are not alone, that the world now knows much more about childhood sexual abuse and its residual effects.

Today, when I experience intruding thoughts, such as being in Maskell's office, I start baking and I feel like my precious mother is there right by my side, letting me know it will be Ok. The wonderful smells that fill my kitchen take me back to a time of pure and complete happiness that my mom and I shared so very long ago.

EPILOGUE

AN EXTRAORDINARY VISITOR

In the Fall of 2019, I received a letter from a woman named Pat telling me she had seen me in *The Keepers* and followed the Keough story. Pat wrote that she had known Sister Catherine Cesnik well. They were classmates and friends during their three-year formation period in the School Sisters of Notre Dame. They taught English together at Villa Regina High School for a year. Pat had left the convent in 1967, but was devastated to hear of her dear friend's murder in 1969. She attended the 75th birthday celebration of Sister Cathy on July 22, 2017, a few months after *The Keepers* aired.

In her letter, Pat revealed that she had information I would be interested in, but it didn't involve *The Keepers*, the murder of Sister Cathy or anything about the sex abuse scandal at Keough. She apologized for being so mysterious and asked if I would meet her for coffee. In early December 2019, we met at my home.

Pat brought me her marvelous homemade chicken soup along with an apple cobbler she had prepared to be baked in my oven. The wonderful aroma of the cinnamon spices mingled with the sliced apples in the cobbler and created a friendly homey atmosphere. This, coupled with cheerful Christmas decorations throughout my home, made both of us feel comfortable and relaxed. I laughed as I told Pat how much I enjoyed baking, and we talked as though we had known each other for years. Suddenly, Pat brought up the proverbial elephant in the room. She said she bet I wanted to know what the mysterious information she uncovered, had to do with me. I laughingly responded that I was anxious to hear about it and couldn't wait much longer to learn what she had to say.

Pat told me that she believed we were closely related, that we shared genetic markers. I was always interested in my ancestry and genealogy. I even had birth records and a paternal family tree that my uncle put together for my dad years ago. I asked Pat if she believed we had common ancestors. Pat shook her head yes as she pulled out some papers and her laptop computer. She added that she had submitted her DNA to a reliable online ancestral registry and that Lisa Gagne was identified as her close relative, possibly a 1st cousin. I knew that my daughter Lisa was in the DNA registry that Pat was referring to. I told Pat that Lisa was my oldest daughter. Pat then opened her laptop and showed me her complete DNA match list. I immediately recognized several of my cousins that were listed as sharing genetic markers with Pat. My interest really spiked when I saw that my paternal grandmother, along with her eleven siblings, too, shared significant DNA with Pat. Pat managed to zero in on my paternal grandfather and ultimately his four children, including my father, Joseph B. Harris.

Pat saw that my maiden name was Harris and was able to identify me as the daughter of Joe Harris. She knew who I was from watching The Keepers in which I had revealed my maiden name. Pat was better able to follow the leads on the ancestry site and soon realized that we shared the same father!

Wow! I had a sister! A sister I found through *The Keepers*! I hugged Pat at this point and told her I always wanted a sister. What a gift she was, a wonderful Christmas gift!

I told Pat that I had suspected for many years I had a sibling. She glanced at me, puzzled. I explained that after my dad died, I went through some of his personal documents. He had saved many boxes of his old clients' legal files. Mixed in with these documents were pictures of my dad with some of his old girlfriends. Dad was five years older than my mom and my mom had always told me that he dated girls before meeting her, because she was too young to date at the time. Wow, I thought, she wasn't kidding. Dad appeared to have quite a selection of female friends back in the day.

I went on to explain to Pat that my dad's University of Baltimore law school yearbook had a caption under his graduation picture that said something like, "If you ever want to find Joe, look in the cafeteria--not because Joe is always hungry, but because Bert works there." It was then Pat told me that her mother's name was Roberta, and she went by "Bert." Also tucked in the yearbook was a mysterious doctor's note stating that Bert was three months pregnant around the time my dad was dating her. Taped to that, was a newspaper clipping from several months later announcing the marriage of Roberta to another man. I always wondered why my dad would save such an announcement of his former girlfriend marrying another guy. I told Pat I had taken all my findings to my Uncle and asked him about my dad dating "Bert" in law school. My uncle was surprised to see all of the pictures, notes, and clippings I had found but would only say that my dad and Bert dated for a while.

I led Pat upstairs to my walk-in closet and pulled out an old cardboard box containing my dad's year book among other memorabilia. I pulled out an envelope containing multiple pictures of Dad's old girlfriends and handed it to Pat. As we looked through the tattered black and white pictures, Pat recognized one of her mom with my dad! Dad had his arms around Bert and they appeared to be a couple. Several more photos of Bert and my dad fell from his yearbook as Pat and I carried the memorabilia downstairs to the kitchen table for a closer look.

My thoughts jumped to Pat as I began to feel concerned about how she must feel. She told me she only learned her father wasn't her biological father a few months earlier when her father's sister joined Ancestry, but did not come up as a match for Pat. How shocking that must have been! I could only imagine the flood of emotions Pat had to endure and my heart went out to her.

Pat and I sat at my kitchen table covered with my Christmas tablecloth, decorated with crimson poinsettias, complete with sparkling silver trim. Suddenly, the timer went off indicating the apple cobbler was done, so I suggested we eat and continue looking at the old records after lunch. I set out some soup bowls and dessert plates and Randy joined us for a wonderful lunch. I told Randy that Pat was my sister. He didn't even look surprised. I guess he was used to me telling him outrageous things about my life.

After lunch, Pat and I continued to look through the shabby old box containing the papers that forever changed our lives. To my surprise, Pat grew up very near my childhood home. She had attended St. Bernardine's School. When she was a teenager, her family moved to St. William's parish, a mile and a half "up" Edmondson Avenue, where I went to school. So, we actually could have attended mass together. Our homes were a mile apart—in opposite directions from the church. Pat had biked some of the same streets where I had played as a child. We wondered how many times we must have walked by each other at church. She shared her love of milkshakes at the Arundel at Edmondson Village where I, too, enjoyed them.

Pat occasionally went to the Hunting Hills Swimming pool where I practically lived during the summer months. I told her how much I loved the pool and that I was on the swim team there. She remembered driving by my childhood home on Nottingham Road decades later and her mom saying she knew the man who lived there.

I asked Pat about Sister Cathy and she told me that Sister Cathy was a kind, gentle, and caring person. I felt an extreme peace and calmness as I listened to my new-found sister talk about Sister Cathy. Pat and I discovered that we have many things in common. She is a retired professor, a writer, and enjoys public speaking as do I.

I told Pat that she was a wonderful Christmas gift and that I was so very glad to meet her. We spoke about letting the Keough survivor group know how all this came about from The Keepers documentary and how Pat knew Sister Cathy. This has been an exciting experience for me. I felt that maybe some of the other survivors want to share my positive experience and see something, very wonderful, that came about, partly from exposing the evil that took place at Keough.

Shortly after meeting Pat, I sent my DNA off to the ancestry site and confirmed beyond any doubt that we were half-sisters. There was no question in my mind after I met Pat and reviewed my dad's records, that we were sisters. Now I had scientific DNA confirmation.

After that eventful December day, Pat and I met twice in person and, when COVID restrictions were enacted, emailed each other regularly. We accumulated hundreds of pages of correspondence--sharing stories and stresses, causes and concerns, politics and passions, favorite relaxations and recipes. We are truly on our way to becoming more than DNA sisters!

ACKNOWLEDGEMENTS

I'd like to acknowledge and thank the following people who were instrumental to me with regard to my writing endeavor.

Annette Winter Sudbrook for her ongoing support and dedication from conception to completion of my memoir. For the book's cover design and prologue as well as writing and editing guidance.

Randy Lancaster for his unconditional love and companionship for over three decades.

Christy Gagne for her ideas and ability to lighten the mood throughout the arduous process of writing this book.

Lisa Gagne Holm for her unrelenting support and profound insight with regard to my memoir.

Mark D. Harris MD for his loyalty, always standing by me throughout twelve rigorous years of Catholic schooling, no matter what.

Pat Montley for seeking me out and being the best big sister I could ever dream of and having boundless confidence in me.

Jean Wehner, whose bravery throughout our Doe/Roe case, *The Keepers* and beyond is unsurpassed.

Joan Dantoni Harris for listening to my ideas throughout the daunting months it took for me to write this book and for being the best cousin ever.

Kimberly O'Kane, Esquire for continuously instilling confidence in me.... "You got this."

Anne Copeland for helping me perfect my story by sharing ideas...even into the wee hours of the night.

Patricia Potter for always 'being there' for Linda and me throughout the seemingly endless days of torture at Keough.

Courtney for her caring, continuous support and always having time to discuss my ideas.

Mary Ann for being my dear friend since first grade at St. William of York grammar school and still believing in me.

Gloria Larkin for courageously coming forward to expose the rampant sex abuse at Keough and continuing to fight against the archaic SOL law.

ACKNOWLEDGEMENTS

And Thank you to my *Keepers* family

Jess Hargrave for her upbeat talented manner of bringing out the best in me.

Ryan White for his expertise in delicately conducting interviews about such poignant times.

John Benam for his exceptionally skillful photography combined with genuine concern for my wellbeing.

Gemma Hoskins for her tremendous drive to uncover the truth and providing much- needed support for the survivors while holding compassion in her heart.

Abbie Fitzgerald Schaub for tirelessly researching the facts surrounding the murders of Sister Cathy and Joyce as well as those connected to the abuse at Keough. And for continuing to battle for SOL reform.

Donna for her companionship throughout the filming of *The Keepers* and beyond.

Lil Hughes Knipp for courageously sharing her story in *The Keepers* while offering support for her Keough sisters.

Printed in Great Britain
by Amazon